BLOODAXE POEMS OF THE YEAR
2003

NEIL ASTLEY has been editing and publishing poetry for nearly 30 years. He founded Bloodaxe Books in 1978, and was given a D.Litt by Newcastle University for his pioneering work. He has published several other anthologies, including *Staying Alive: real poems for unreal times*, *Poetry with an Edge*, *New Blood*, *Pleased to See Me: 69 very sexy poems* and *Do Not Go Gentle: poems for funerals*, as well as two collections, *Darwin Survivor* (Poetry Book Society Recommendation) and *Biting My Tongue*. He won an Eric Gregory Award for his own poetry. His novel *The End of My Tether* was shortlisted for the Whitbread First Novel Award in 2002, and has just been published in paperback by Scribner.

BLOODAXE
POEMS OF THE YEAR
2003

edited by
NEIL ASTLEY

BLOODAXE BOOKS

ISBN: 1 85224 654 5

First published 2003 by
Bloodaxe Books Ltd,
Highgreen,
Tarset,
Northumberland NE48 1RP.

www.bloodaxebooks.com
For further information about Bloodaxe titles
please visit our website or write to
the above address for a catalogue.

Bloodaxe Books Ltd acknowledges
the financial assistance of
Arts Council England, North East.

Printed in Great Britain by
Bell & Bain Limited, Glasgow, Scotland.

CONTENTS

PREFACE

Bloodaxe Books celebrates its 25th birthday in 2003. This sampler anthology marks the quarter century with poems from 25 new books published in the anniversary year. Sadly, this year has also seen the death of Ken Smith. His pamphlet *Tristan Crazy* was Bloodaxe's first publication in October 1978, the first of a dozen titles he published with Bloodaxe over 25 years. This anthology opens with a poem from that sequence, followed by a selection from Ken Smith's second retrospective, *Shed: Poems 1980-2001*, published in 2002. Always an outsider – but a central figure in any balanced account of postwar British poetry – Ken Smith wouldn't have relished the irony that after his most important book received no reviews at all (in the national press last year) the papers have now lamented his passing and honoured his work with lengthy tributes.

Bringing Ken Smith's work to the attention of a wider readership was one of Bloodaxe's first editorial objectives. He was one of many poets whose work has been much appreciated by readers but not by (the arbiters of critical taste) When Ken returned from America in 1973, he found himself out of favour with British editors because his poetry went against the grain of (publishers' lists still dominated by writers from The Movement and The Group) Now there are two substantial Ken Smith selections in print covering 40 years of his writing, but his poetry remains marginalised, latterly because the politically edgy, colloquially-styled work which inspired the new British poets of the 80s and 90s is too plain-speaking, too cussed and off-the-wall to be taken seriously (by today's critical fraternity.)

A publisher's 25th birthday should be an occasion for celebration, but any sense of personal achievement I feel in having helped open up a wider readership for poetry in Britain has been dampened by the recent emergence of (poetry's new academic spin doctors.) The puritanical members of that (bogus male cult of literary seriousness and poetic difficulty) are now publicly trashing any writer or book perceived as threatening their (critical policing of contemporary poetry) from the wonderful American poet Billy Collins (scorned as 'sentimental') to Bloodaxe's *Staying Alive* anthology ('definitively dreadful'). With women writers their tactic involves either offhand dismissal (so Anne Stevenson's poetry is 'maudlin' and 'bad writing') or simply ignoring their publications (the latest issue of *Poetry Review* features reviews of 21 new titles, only *one* of these by a woman, an avant-gardist).

It seems that the poetry clock has turned full circle. When I founded Bloodaxe 25 years ago, I saw myself as a representative reader. I wanted to overturn Adrian Mitchell's dictum that *Most people ignore most poetry because most poetry ignores most people*, having realised that there were many different kinds of poetry being written which *didn't* ignore people, but that much of it wasn't being published. Publishers weren't serving readers. Even now there's still a mismatch between publication and readership: over three-quarters of poetry collections published by the main imprints are by men, despite the fact that poetry's readership is over two-thirds female, and numerous women poets are either unpublished or only available in small press editions not found in bookshops) And the published women poets receive far less review coverage than the men.

With many poetry editors paying more heed to peer approval) than reader response, and (poetry's sly spin doctors) trying to foist their academically distorted version of contemporary poetry on baffled readers) it's not surprising that bookshops see poetry as a minority interest. (Intellectual snobbery) has given unwitting support to the profit-driven stocking policies of the main bookselling chains. Big reductions made to the range and size of their poetry sections have had a knock-on effect on publishers, who have had to restrict the numbers of new poets and new titles they are taking on. But publishers who have tried to counter this trend by using imaginative design (with straightforward commentary) to take books of accessible contemporary poetry to a broader readership have been berated by (snooty poet-reviewers for 'patronising' intelligent readers) (our bulging postbag proves otherwise) and even for 'mixing poetry with promotional culture' and 'promoting poetry as fashion statement'. Thus *Staying Alive* was somewhat confusingly denigrated as 'an anthology that could have been great if it wasn't being sold as a kind of lavender bath oil for the brain (i.e. this poetry does you good)' which is a bit like saying that *Pride and Prejudice* would have been a great novel if it hadn't been adapted for television.)

The fact that *Staying Alive* became Britain's top poetry title last year offended (all those poetry snobs) who believe that the best way to keep poetry (exclusively male and fashionably intellectual) is not to sell poetry books to the wider public. Every review of this popular anthology by non-poets was genuinely appreciative (both John Carey and Ian Rankin called it 'a revelation'), but *all* the negative reviews – and there were many scathing ones – were by (disdainful male poets (whose own poetry would be incomprehensible to anyone not versed in late 20th century postmodernism)

The agenda behind such attacks is that (these men believe poetry's prime concern is language (for its own sake) and intellectual play, not communication and human life) And because they are clever and articulate young men – adept at veiling their elitism and misogynistic attitudes behind a pretence of critical authority – they've taken over many key positions of literary influence without many people realising that their aesthetic arguments are not only spurious but dangerous. Readers already familiar with books they misrepresent aren't taken in by their plausible criticism, but many are given the impression that books they would actually find rewarding are 'bad writing', and so don't buy them; and booksellers are led to believe that such titles aren't worth stocking.

As well as the 25 collections featured in this sampler, Bloodaxe is also publishing five anthologies in 2003, including Maura Dooley's *The Honey Gatherers: a book of love poems*, Peter Forbes's *We Have Come Through: 100 poems celebrating courage in overcoming depression and trauma* (published with Survivors' Poetry) and my anthology *Do Not Go Gentle: poems for funerals*. Like *Staying Alive*, these are all books of poetry for people, aimed not only at serving poetry's existing readership but at showing new readers that much contemporary poetry is imaginatively adventurous, humanly aware, spiritually sustaining and 'strong enough to help' (George Seferis).

A book which includes only poets from one publishing house cannot show the whole spectrum of contemporary poetry, but an anthology from a publisher with a list as diverse as Bloodaxe's must be more representative of 21st century poetry than the narrow picture presented by those intellectual bigots from the poetry police. They will hate it of course, but this book's true readers will be open-minded and eager to read work by the many different kinds of poets represented in these pages. I hope my selection will stimulate interest in many of the featured titles.

Since 1978 Bloodaxe has published over 700 books by more than 300 writers. In any year the proportion of poets published from Britain and other countries will vary. In 2003 there are eight titles by poets from North America, six translations and one first collection by a new British poet, but in 2004 there will be fewer Americans and three or more first collections. These are all "risky" books in publishing terms: although readers are interested in poetry from around the world and collections by new writers, these kinds of books aren't available in many bookshops because they rarely receive much review coverage. Without grant-aid, it would not be possible to serve our readership by publishing such a wide range of new writing, and we are enormously grateful to Northern Arts and Arts Council England for their continuing support over two decades.

NEIL ASTLEY

Ken Smith (1938-2003)
A TRIBUTE

KEN SMITH was the first poet published by Bloodaxe Books. The first poem here is from that first Bloodaxe title, *Tristan Crazy* (1978) – reprinted in his first retrospective, *The Poet Reclining: Selected Poems 1962-1980*. The others are from his second selection, *Shed: Poems 1980-2001* (2002).

'Ken Smith, who has died, aged 64, was a great poet…Ken Smith simply lived to write, and he was at the height of his powers when he brought Legionnaire's Disease back to London after a visit to Cuba. His last retrospective collection, *Shed*, published in 2002, confirmed the immense power of his poetry.' – JON GLOVER, *The Guardian*, 3 July 2003

'A classic outsider figure, who became a mentor and model for the "New Generation" of British poets that emerged in the 1990s, Ken Smith was a poet of extensive gifts whose intellectual energy took him into a deeper and wider engagement with the world than many of his contemporaries. The first writer-in-residence at a British prison, and a vivid commentator on the emerging New Europe that followed the taking down of the Berlin Wall, Smith was an explorer of people and places whose work gave voice to the sufferings of the marginalised and the unconsidered…The 500 and more pages of his two volumes of selected poems will remain a testament to an exceptionally persistent vision.'
  – OBITUARY: 'Poet whose ever broadening scope and political involvement were an inspiration to a generation', *The Times*, 2 July 2003

'Ken Smith brought an original and memorable voice to poetry in Britain. He spent his writing life not so much swimming against the tide as ignoring the stream's existence. Now he leaves a large and richly varied body of work, some of which will surely outlast that of more fashionable names… He was one of those by whom the language lives.'
  – SEAN O'BRIEN, *The Independent*, 2 July 2003

KEN SMITH was a major voice in world poetry, a writer whose work shifted territory with time, from land to city, from Yorkshire, America and London to the war-ravaged Balkans and Eastern Europe (before and after Communism). He was dubbed 'the godfather of the new poetry' because his work and example influenced and inspired a whole generation of younger British poets. He was writer-in-residence at Wormwood Scrubs prison in 1985-87. In 1997 he received America's highly prestigious Lannan Literary Award for Poetry – one of few British poets given this honour – and then a Cholmondeley Award in 1998.

Smith's first book, *The Pity*, appeared in 1967, and his second, *Work, distances/poems*, from Chicago in 1972. His early books span a transition from his preoccupation with land and myth (when he lived in Yorkshire,

Devon and America) to his later engagement with urban Britain and the politics of radical disaffection (when he lived in East London). *The Poet Reclining: Selected Poems 1962-1980* (1982) covers the first half of his writing career, including the pivotal *Fox Running*; his short prose is collected in *A Book of Chinese Whispers* (1987).

His collections *Terra* (1986), *Wormwood* (1987), *The heart, the border* (1990) and *Tender to the Queen of Spain* (1993) were Poetry Book Society Recommendations. *Terra* was shortlisted for the Whitbread Poetry Award, and his last separate collection, *Wild Root* (1998), a Poetry Book Society Choice, was shortlisted for the T.S. Eliot Prize. All five are included in his second Bloodaxe retrospective, *Shed: Poems 1980-2001* (2002).

Ken Smith was born in rural Yorkshire, the son of an itinerant Irish farm labourer. The first poem evokes the boy in the raw landscape of his childhood as well as the grown-up man looking back at his life, examining his relationship with a difficult father. The poem from *Hawkwood*, about a medieval mercenary, is also a self-portrait of the journeyman writer.

Being the third song of Urias

Lives ago, years past generations
perhaps nowhere I dreamed it:
the foggy ploughland of wind
and hoofprints, my father
off in the mist topping beets.

Where I was eight, I knew nothing,
the world a cold winter light
on half a dozen fields, then
all the winking blether of stars.

Before like a fool I began
explaining the key in its lost locked box
adding words to the words to the sum
that never works out.

           Where I was
distracted again by the lapwing,
the damp morning air of my father's
gregarious plainchant cursing
all that his masters deserved
and had paid for.
           Sure I was
then for the world's mere being
in the white rime on weeds

among the wet hawthorn berries
at the field's edge darkened by frost,
and none of these damned words to say it.

I began trailing out there in voices,
friends, women, my children,
my father's tetherless anger, some
like him who are dead who are
part of the rain now.

Years go by
(FROM *Poem without a title*)

Father I say. Dad? You again?
I take your arm, your elbow,
I turn you around in the dark and I say

go back now, you're sleepwalking again,
you're talking out loud again, talking in tongues
and your dream is disturbing my dream.

And none of this is any of your apples,
and even now as the centuries begin to happen
I can say: go away, you and all your violence.

Shush, now, old man.
Time to go back to your seat in the one-and-nines,
to your black bench on the Esplanade,

your name and your dates on a metal plate, back
to your own deckchair on the pier, your very own
kitchen chair tipped back on the red kitchen tiles

and you asleep, your feet up on the brass fender
and the fire banked, your cheek cocked
to the radio set, this is the 9 o'clock news Dad.

It's time. It's long past it.
Time to go back up the long pale corridor
there's no coming back from.

from Hawkwood

Seated, a man with the tools of his trade,
solitary in the company of weapons,
always the warrior, apart,
etched into metal in a moment of brooding.

Mostly he sleeps sound till first light,
by day lives the life of his time:
fighting to live he will fight
for cash money or credit. Or not fight.

At his ease when he may be,
who can never go home now,
his landscape the blunt northerly speech
glimpsed through the window to his left

where the hills are already going to sleep,
the road hatched away into more shadow
always closing round him. In the foreground
a single candle he has lit against the night.

In the next street

There's only ever one argument: his,
bawling out whoever punctuates
the brief intervals his cussing
interrupts, something unheard, reason perhaps.

What you never get is silence,
always some groan on the horizon
out on the borders of attention
where would be quiet if they let it.

Always some conversation far away,
foreign, banal, dramatic, translated
it means *my wife's name is Judit.*
I am an engineer from Spidertown.

What to reply? *Your Majesty*
my name is Smith. All lies anyway,
all we do is get drunk, the evening's end
collapsing loosely into gutturals.

We drink to silence, where the stars think.
We drink to the music of rain on the roof.
We drink to mothers, brothers, lovers, kids,
to the candle burning down its length

till someone blows it out. Distance
makes no difference, the same want
for love and money, the numbers of the winning line
in the state lottery like a needle in the brain.

And then I've had enough. I want
to go home now, far away, plug myself
back into the sockets, the blackbird,
the evening humming stories to itself.

Everything in its place, the moths,
the mouse in the mousetrap. And
in the next street the same old argument.
He's sure he's right.

Malenki robot

(for János, Nagyszelmenc, Slovakia)

'Over there in the other country
my sister had daughters I've seen once
in forty years, nor visited my dead.
It's too late now, they're poor there,
and here I'm just an old working man,
and the only thing left for me to do is die.

'These are my blunt carpenter's hands,
and this on their backs the frost
that gnawed them at Szolyva, three winters,
two years I was a prisoner there.
Monday I build doors, Tuesday put on roofs.
Roofs. Doors. My life. Vodka.

It was the priest told me to go,
three days he said, a little light work,
malenki robot, two years building roofs,
and that because I had a trade.
I survived wearing the clothes of those who died,
after a while I survived because I had survived,
and then came home and here the border.'

The wire runs through the heart, dammit,
therefore we will drink cheap Russian vodka
in János' kitchen, and later take a walk
down to the border and look back
into the other world, the village in the mirror
that is the other half of us, here,
where the street stops at the wire
and goes on again on the other side,
and maybe the Gypsies will come to serenade us.

Here

I point to where the pain is, the ache
where the blockage is. Here.
The doctor shakes his head at me. Yes
he says, I have that, we all have.

They put the wire in again, on the monitor
I watch the grey map of my heart, the bent
ladder of the spine that outlasts it.
How does it feel? they ask. Here?

I am moving away down the long corridors
of abandoned trolleys, the closed wings
of hospitals, rooms full of yellow bedpans
and screens and walker frames, fading out

into nothing and nothing at all, as we do,
as we all do, as it happens, and no one
can talk of it. Here, where the heart
dies, where all the systems are dying.

Anne Stevenson
A Report from the Border
POETRY BOOK SOCIETY RECOMMENDATION

3 January 2003 (Anne Stevenson's 70th birthday)

ANNE STEVENSON was born in 1933 in Cambridge of American parents, grew up in the US and has lived in Britain for most of her life. Her other books include *Collected Poems 1955-1995* and *Granny Scarecrow* (2000).

Anne Stevenson's new collection crosses many borders. While her title-poem mocks borders dividing rich nations from poor, its subtext undermines the public language of political self-justification, suggesting that the true dimensions of morality can be approached best through literature. Many of these poems balance between youth and age, life and death, love and friendship, science and mythology, terrorists and victims.

As always, her poems are sharp-edged, disconcerting and musical, often bordering on laughter or tears. Never trying/sell ideas or confirm prejudices, she reveals – through scrupulous choice of language – profound, complex, hidden, maybe shaming but certainly important insights into human nature.

A Report from the Border

Wars in peacetime don't behave like wars.
So loving they arc.
Kissed on both cheeks, silk-lined ambassadors
Pose and confer.

Unbuckle your envy, drop it there by the door.
We will settle,
We will settle without blows or bullets
The unequal score.

In nature, havenots have to be many
And havelots few.
Making money out of making money
Helps us help you.

This from the party of useful words. From the other,
Hunger's stare,
Drowned crops, charred hopes, fear, stupor, prayer
And literature.

Who's Joking with the Photographer?
(Photographs of myself approaching seventy)

Not my final face, a map of how to get there.
Seven ages, seven irreversible layers, each
subtler and more supple than a snake's skin.
Nobody looks surprised when we slough off one
and begin to inhabit another.
Do we exchange them whole in our sleep, or
are they washed away in pieces, cheek by brow by chin,
in the steady abrasions of the solar shower?
Draw first breath, and time turns on its taps.
No wonder the newborn's tiny face crinkles and cries:
chill, then a sharp collision with light,
the mouth's desperation for the foreign nipple,
all the uses of eyes, ears, hands still to be learned
before the self pulls away in its skin-tight sphere
to endure on its own the tectonic geology of childhood.

Imagine in space-time irretrievable mothers viewing
the pensioners their babies have become.
'Well, that's life, nothing we can do about it now.'
They don't love us as much as they did, and
why should they? We have replaced them. Just as we're
being replaced by big sassy kids in school blazers.
Meanwhile, Federal Express has delivered my sixth face –
grandmother's, scraps of me grafted to her bones.
I don't believe it. Who made this mess,
this developer's sprawl of roads that can't be retaken,
high tension wires that run dangerously under the skin?
What is it the sceptical eyes are saying to the twisted lips:
ambition is a cliché, beauty a banality? In any case,
this face has given them up – old friends whose obituaries
it reads in the mirror with scarcely a regret.

So, who's joking with the photographer?
And what did she think she was doing,
taking pictures of the impossible? Was a radioscope
attached to her lens? Something teasing under the skull
has infiltrated the surface, something you can't see
until you look away, then it shoots out and tickles you.
You could call it soul or spirit, but that would be serious.

Look for a word that mixes affection with insurrection,
frivolity, child's play, rude curiosity,
a willingness to lift the seventh veil and welcome Yorick.
That's partly what the photo says. The rest is private,
guilt that rouses memory at four in the morning,
truths such as Hamlet used, torturing his mother,
all the dark half-tones of the sensuous unsayable
finding a whole woman there, in her one face.

A Marriage

When my mother knew why her treatment wasn't working,
She said to my father, trying not to detonate her news,
'Steve, you must marry again. When I'm gone, who's going
To tell you to put your trousers on before your shoes?'

My father opened his mouth to — couldn't — refuse.
Instead, he threw her a look, a man just shot
Gazing at the arm or leg he was about to lose.
His cigarette burned him, but he didn't stub it out.

Later, on the porch, alive in the dark together,
How solid the house must have felt, how sanely familiar
The street-lit leaves, their shadows patterning the street.
The house is still there. The elms and the people, not.

It was now, and it never was now. Like every experience
Of being entirely here, yet really not being.
They couldn't imagine the future that I am seeing,
For all his philosophy and all her common sense.

Esta Spalding
Anchoress

January 2003

ESTA SPALDING was born in 1966. She has published four books of poetry in Canada, edited *The Griffin Poetry Prize Anthology*, and is co-editor of *Brick: A Literary Journal* and of *Lost Classics* (Bloomsbury, 2000). She lives in Vancouver.

A sensual, haunting book-length poem by a highly original Canadian poet and novelist, *Anchoress* is set during the 1991 Gulf War. This remarkable book challenges the way we think about the boundaries between politics and passion, war and love, fiction and poetry.

A year after Helen's death, Peter begins to assemble memories of his lover. But how to conjure the dead? How to put a lover's body together again? In his laboratory Peter is restoring the skeleton of a whale. But in his notebook, he scrawls pieces of Helen's story and of their lives together. Slowly, he begins to see the secret tunnels between Helen's death and the deaths of her parents, between Helen's loyalty to her sister and her passion for right action. *Anchoress* moves gracefully from the painted caves of Vichy France where Helen's mother is born, to the banks of the Seine where her parents meet; from a foster home to the university where Helen becomes obsessed with the televised events of the Gulf War.

from Anchoress

Because what she believed was
big enough for this world – or it was

too small, something anyone
could pack in an overnight bag, strap on
a back, carry at the end of a stick (not even
drooping under the weight), because

it was dangerous, incendiary,
uninspected. Because those who could strike
the match were miles away, boarding
helicopters, hugging wives, sons, daughters,
waving to the crowd (with closed fingers),
were in choppers lifting off from aircraft carriers
(stirring up the brine – the names of the dead

lifting off the waves towards them
in a speech they cannot interpret),

because what she believed crawled
in her belly, rumbling through
the tunnels in her body, shaking her skin
(I put my hand on her wrist
and felt it),
it was not satisfied by rhetoric.

Because it was beautiful
and she fed it.

*

A painted ibex
in the headlights,
a whale in an ice
sheet, frozen

by her love. Nothing
like her had ever touched me before,
I was in a cavern whose markings I did not recognise.
No recipes.
Colours from a different spectrum.
It was blood inventing channels into new life,
it stung. The way life stings.
The way it hurts to eat when you've been
hungry.

When a despot wants to starve the people
he does not burn their rice, he breaks
their cooking pots.

I came to her without a vessel.

*

Students thick in the quadrangles,
the sun lecherous
on the white stone buildings, that grey city,
mound of bones, she squats below
the flagpole, dog chain around her neck

and hung from it the sign, *Peace,*
she means this, lifting the heavy metal
canister and bending her neck forward,
as a woman washing her hair will bend
her neck forward, her hair falling over her face

she soaks in gasoline, pours it down her neck,
heavy canister, sloshing gas on her back,
ribbons of gasoline
splash on her jeans, her feet, the snow
on the ground catches it
in pools that rainbow around her, furious
birds overhead, and squirrels, feeding,
oblivious

*

Helen's poem

My feet are for burning,
are for burning, to send up an SOS.

My back is for burning,
is for burning, a signal flare, a promise.

My face is for sweet burning,
is for sweet burning, my only gift.

And I am for burning, a black candle lit for you.

*

On fire, dancing. Everyone could see
her eyes, their screaming, someone ran to her
released the rope from the pole
wrapped her electric body
in the flag.

*

FABIENNE BROCHIER

Julia Copus
In Defence of Adultery
POETRY BOOK SOCIETY RECOMMENDATION
February 2003

JULIA COPUS (*b.* 1969) won the National Poetry Competition in 2003. Her first book *The Shuttered Eye* (Poetry Book Society Recommendation) was shortlisted for the Forward Prize for Best First Collection in 1995.

'We don't fall in love: it rises through us / the way that certain music does,' writes Julia Copus in her title-poem. So too these quirky, highly musical poems infuse and stir us as we read them, sharing her unease and anxiety with a sense of personal recognition. Imbued with a wry logic and a spellbinding resonance, *In Defence of Adultery* traces the paths of lives and relationships through a world carved out by the choices we make. At the same time, it summons up another world beneath our ever-pressing turmoil of love and family relationships, a parallel world made up of what might have been, as well as what might still be. Dense, elliptical and suggestive, these vital poems hold science and art, time and timelessness in a tense balance.

In Defence of Adultery

We don't fall in love: it rises through us
the way that certain music does –
whether a symphony or ballad –
and it is sepia-coloured,
like spilt tea that inches up
the tiny tube-like gaps inside
a cube of sugar lying by a cup.
Yes, love's like that: just when we least
needed or expected it
a part of us dips into it
by chance or mishap and it seeps
through our capillaries, it clings
inside the chambers of the heart.
We're victims, we say: mere vessels,
drinking the vanilla scent
of this one's skin, the lustre
of another's eyes so skilfully
darkened with bistre. And whatever
damage might result we're not

23

to blame for it: love is an autocrat
and won't be disobeyed.
Sometimes we manage
to convince ourselves of that.

Love, Like Water

Tumbling from some far-flung cloud
into your bathroom alone, to sleeve
a toe, five toes, a metatarsal arch,
it does its best to feign indifference
to the body, but will go on creeping
up to the neck till it's reading the skin
like braille, though you're certain it sees
under the surface of things and knows
the routes your nerves take as they branch
from the mind, which lately has been curling
in on itself like the spine of a dog
as it circles a patch of ground to sleep.
Now through the dappled window,
propped open slightly for the heat,
a light rain is composing
the lake it falls into, the way a lover's hand
composes the body it touches – Love,
like water! How it gives and gives,
wearing the deepest of grooves in our sides
and filling them up again, ever so gently
wounding us, making us whole.

Breaking the Rule

I *The Art of Illumination*

At times it is a good life, with the evening sun
gilding the abbey tower, the cold brook

sliding past and every hour in my Book
a blank page, vellum pumiced

24

to a lustre, so the inks won't spread –
saffron and sandarach and dragon's blood,

azure and verdigris. Monsters and every type of beast
curl round the words. Each man here has a past,

and each man reasons for his faith.
I wronged a woman once.

My floor is strewn with thyme and rosemary
to mask the odours – fish glue, resins

vinegar and oils. With these I draw
the hosts of the redeemed, and every face

takes on the features of a face I've known
and every angel's face beneath the shadow

of its many-coloured wings is hers alone.

II *The Art of Signing*

There are ways among the stone and shadow
to transgress the Rule. We speak

in signs: a language with no grammar.
For the sign of bread you make a circle

with your thumbs and index fingers – like the belt
that pressed the silk against her waist.

For an eel, you place one fist on top of another,
as if grasping a cord of hair to kiss

that one mouth only in the frantic din
of the ale-house, where we used to dance,

and later outside in the grainy dusk
our four feet shuffling over the quiet earth.

For the sign of silence put a finger
to the dry muscle of your mouth,

the darkness that's inside it. Keep it there.

Brendan Kennelly
Martial Art
April 2003

BRENDAN KENNELLY (*b.* 1936) is Professor of Modern Literature at Trinity College Dublin, and has published 15 other titles with Bloodaxe. MARTIAL (*c.* 40-104 AD) was born in Spain but spent most of his life in Rome, railing against its people and society.

The Roman satirist Martial is brought up to date by a partner in mischief in Brendan Kennelly's *Martial Art*. He is a satirist trying to define generosity, happiness and love – with scurrilous candour and piercing clarity – in brief punchy poems. But no matter how savage his attacks, he is always playful and compassionate. He is a sharp, visionary writer who knows the world about him and is in touch with the world within himself, at once bewildered, attentive and bitingly articulate.

Brendan Kennelly: 'If he'd been a boxer, he'd have developed a new kind of knockout punch, smiling at his victim as he walked back to his corner...Is one translating Martial? Or is Martial, smiling and mischievous as ever, translating the translator?'

Three things

Three things make an epigram sing:
brevity, honey, sting.

How it is

Some of my poems are good, some
not up to scratch, some
bad.

That's how it is with most books,
if the truth were told.

Who tells the truth about truth, my dear?
Make way for the judge and the jester.

Nothing

You say my epigrams are too long.
Yours are shorter.
You write nothing.

Brevity

This writer of couplets is bent on brevity.
What's the good of brevity
if his couplets fill a book?

I Hear

I hear Cinna has written some verses against me.

A man is no writer
if his poems have no reader.

Pleasure

What's the point of writing things, Sextus,
which few people begin to understand?
Your books need a clever, interpreting god,
not an ordinary reader. You think
Cinna a better writer than Virgil.
On the basis of such thinking, may your works
receive equal praise. As for myself, Sextus,
I hope my verse gives pleasure to critics,
provided it gives pleasure to other people
without the help of such insightful souls.

I want you, Loftus

I run from your table, Loftus,
splendid and all as it is, rich
with the choicest food and drink.
When you recite, you ruin it all.
I don't want you to set before me
turbot, mullet, salmon or trout.
I don't want your mushrooms or your oysters.
I want you, Loftus, to keep your mouth shut.

Muffler

Why do you wrap that muffler around your neck
when you're going to recite poems to us visitors?
The muffler is better suited to our ears.

The reason

You ask me why I like the country air.
I never meet you there.

Nothing left

You had four teeth left. A bad cough got rid of two.
Another fit and the other two were gone.
Laugh away to blazes now. There's nothing left
for a third fit of coughing to do.

Sarah Wardle
Fields Away

SHORTLISTED FOR THE FORWARD PRIZE
FOR BEST FIRST COLLECTION

April 2003

SARAH WARDLE (*b.* 1969) won the Geoffrey Dearmer Prize in 1999. She lives near Rye in East Sussex, and teaches at Middlesex University. *Fields Away* is her first collection.

Sarah Wardle's poetry ranges from playful wit to gentle lyrics, exploring a personal geography from country to city. Every poem covers different territory, but in each the voice is distinctively hers: 'sparky and feisty' (Sheenagh Pugh), with 'a hint of darkness and wicked wit' (Roddy Lumsden). She can be mischievously inventive as well as powerfully reflective, and 'she can open philosophical puzzles or illuminate the commonplace and local' (Michael Donaghy). She writes with penetrating insight and sensitivity about acute illness and recovery, in poems such as 'Digitalis' and 'Flight', in which we watch her, like the released blackbird, 'spread her wings and soar'. 'In her work it is always the poem that impresses, not the poet,' says Hugo Williams.

Flight

The mother blackbird I've been feeding
has flown in the open door of the kitchen,
where she flutters against the stuck window,
like a butterfly, finding no way through.

A startled eye stares. In the flap of a wing
it all comes back: my heart beating
so fast I thought it would explode,
my mind and body in overload,

running the corridors, fleeing nurses,
who seemed stranger than another species,
then trapped in a room with nowhere to go,
how I was cornered at a safety window,

which opened only far enough for air,
how I didn't know there was no cause to fear,
how they outnumbered me, fastened their grip,
laid me down and injected me, like rape.

I cup the bird gently in my hands, like water,
carry her out, as if a Section order
has been lifted, give her to the air,
then watch her spread her wings and soar.

Digitalis

As a child I used to sift
through batches of grass
for four-leaf clovers.

Each three-headed stem
on the factory floor
looked the same as the others.

That summer a bee
must have cross-pollinated
a foxglove and hollyhock.

The freak flower stood tall,
despite being stuck
in nature's cul-de-sac.

Its petals opened wide,
a satellite dish
receiving strange radar,

ultrasonic waves,
the likes of which
most gardens can't hear.

I marvelled at it,
unaware I was growing
up schizophrenic,

neither better nor worse
than anybody else,
just different.

The Close

Where do they live, the sounds of other people,
the boy who plays his trumpet out of key,
the woman talking at her kitchen table,
the snatch of a tennis match on TV,

the sprinkler on a lawn, set to stop and go,
the dog that barks whenever it is bored,
the music from a curtained upstairs window,
the wood pigeon which plays its stuck record?

Where do they live, in or outside you?
You ask till you no longer want to know,
because you can hear your own footsteps too,
and the silence of your shadow on the road.

Lesson, 1914

What form is the adjective in sentence one?
Well done, Jones. The *bravest* soldiers won.

Why did they go to war? Sentence two.
That's right. It was *necessary* to.

Look at the verb. Who fights in sentence three?
Yes, Watson. First person plural: *we*.

Now, which tense is used in sentence four?
Good. We *shall* be victorious in the war.

How many will have perished? Sentence five.
Excellent. *A great host* will have died.

GOLBARG ZOLFAGHARI

Kapka Kassabova
Someone else's life
April 2003

KAPKA KASSABOVA was born in 1973 and grew up in Sofia. Since 1990 she has lived in England, France, Germany and New Zealand. Her book includes work from two New Zealand collections as well as new poems. She has also published two novels with Penguin.

Kapka Kassabova is a young Bulgarian émigré poet who writes in English but with a European imagination. In *Someone else's life* she explores the emotional and spiritual territory of the traveller and the dispossessed, the spaces between memory and being, exploration and doubt, desire and loss. Clive James has praised her 'finely pitched lyricism' and 'richness of sympathy'. Mark Strand admires her poetry's 'supreme clarity and fearless candor' and 'skeptical, riveting, passionate' intelligence: 'It is a book of perpetual exile, of endless comings and goings, in a world that offers neither stability, nor salvation.'

Place

This is why we come

To wake up to the crowing of plucked roosters
from a sepia childhood

To watch the merging of dawn and dusk,
as matter-of-fact as a lesson in evanescence.

To see without a warning white herons in the bay
still with rarity, guarding their reflection.

To spot a hooded figure on the hill in a yellow raincoat,
in a flashback of self-recognition.

To lie, then stand and fall into the deep storm
from a great height, emerging on the other side of here.

To sleep and when you wake up, to remember it
as something that did not exist, and that will never be again.

This is why we leave.

The Door

One day you'll see:
you've been knocking on a door
without a house.
You've been waiting, shivering, yelling
words of daring and hope.

One day you'll see:
there is no one on the other side
except as ever, the jubilant ocean
that won't shatter ceramically like a dream
when you and I shatter.

But not yet. Now
you wait outside, watching
the blue arches of mornings
that will break
but are now perfect.

Underneath on tiptoe
pass the faces, speaking to you,
saying 'you', 'you', 'you',
smiling, waving, arriving
in unfailing chronology.

One day you'll doubt your movements,
you will shudder
at the accuracy of your sudden age.
You will ache for slow beauty
to save you from your quick, quick life.

But not yet. Hope
fills the yawn of time.
Blue surrounds you. Now let's say
you see a door and knock,
and wait for someone to hear.

And they were both right

There is so much violence yet to be done.
He falls into her body
blind because desire makes him blind
deaf and limbless for the same reason.

But what is love?
And is this a question or a statement?

He will be
undone by it, she shudders in jubilation,
and pulls him to her night – like a dress
to be undone.

Love will be made and unmade – naturally,
unnaturally. It will be invoked
like a reason, like a form of life.
It will be forgotten.

What if love is no more than
a tangle of muscles
aching to be untied
by knowing fingers?

What if love is made and nothing else –
asked Narcissus, leaning over the green iris of water.

Nothing else,
cried Echo from the green cochlea of the woods.

And they were both right.
And they were both lonely.

Carolyn Forché
Blue Hour
April 2003

CAROLYN FORCHÉ (*b*. 1951) has published three books of poetry in Britain. *The Angel of History* (Bloodaxe, 1994) won *The Los Angeles Times* Book Award. Her other books include *Against Forgetting: 20th Century Poetry of Witness* (Norton, 1993).

Carolyn Forché is one of America's most important contemporary poets. *Blue Hour* is a visionary book, and includes *On Earth*, a extraordinary long poem, a meditation on human existence and life on earth. Robert Boyers calls it an elusive book 'because it is ever in pursuit of what the German poet Novalis called the lost presence beyond appearance. The longest poem, *On Earth*, is a transcription of mind passing from life into death, in the form of an abecedary, modeled on ancient gnostic hymns...The hunger to know is matched here by a desire to be new, totally without cynicism, open to the shocks of experience as if perpetually for the first time, though un-illusioned, wise beyond any possible taint of a false or assumed innocence.'

Prayer

Begin again among the poorest, moments off, in another time and place.
Belongings gathered in the last hour, visible invisible:
Tin spoon, teacup, tremble of tray, carpet hanging from sorrow's
       balcony.
Say goodbye to everything. With a wave of your hand, gesture to
       all you have known.
Begin with bread torn from bread, beans given to the hungriest, a
       carcass of flies.
Take the polished stillness from a locked church, prayer notes left
       between stones.
Answer them and hoist in your net voices from the troubled hours.
Sleep only when the least among them sleeps, and then only until
       the birds.
Make the flatbed truck your time and place. Make the least daily
       wage your value.
Language will rise then like language from the mouth of a still river.
       No one's mouth.
Bring night to your imaginings. Bring the darkest passage of your
       holy book.

from **On Earth**

a barnloft of horse dreams, with basin and bedclothes
a bit of polished quiet from a locked church
a black coat in smoke
a black map of clouds on a lake

a blackened book-leaf, straw and implements
a blue daybook hidden in my bed with his name
a branch weighted with pears

a brittle crack of dawnlight
a broken clock, a boy wakened by his father's whip, then the world
        as if whorled into place —

a broken equation, a partita
a bullet clicking through her hair
a bullet-holed supper plate
a burnt room strewn with toy tanks
a century passing through it

a chaos of microphones
a city a thousand years
a city shaken and snowing

a coin of moonlight on the shattered place
a confusion of birds and fishes
a consciousness not within us
a corpse broken into many countries
a cup of sleep
a desire to live as long as the world itself

a door opening another door
a feather forced through black accordioned paper
a field of birds roasted by the heavens
a goodness that must forget itself
a grave strewn with slipper flowers
a groundskeeper's knowledge of graves

a hole in light, an entrance
a horse grazing in an imaginary field
a horse of wire, wine-corks and wax

a horse tangled in its tether
a hotel haunted by a wedding dress
a house fallen in
a house fallen into itself
a house in time, years from the others, light-roofed, walls shimmering

a hurried life, a knife on newsprint
a lace of recent snow

a language known only to parrots
a life in which nothing is lived
a light, n'y voir que du bleu, blind to something
a litany of broken but remembered events

a little hotel in the city with its windows open
a little invention for sweeping crumbs from the table
a locket's parted lovers face to face

a man repainting his wooden house in stopped time
a man vanishing while he danced
a man who built cottages for tourists until he went blind

a memory through which one hasn't lived
a message deflected by other messages
a message from a secret self

a mist of geese rising
a moment of bluesmoke
a moment of sycamores in low mist
a moon caught in the bare hold of firs
a moon haloed in high cirrus

a name which should not be written
a new world, entirely other
a no-longer-beyond

a parcel of copper wire, plastique and a clock
a parrot learning its language from a ghost
a past to come

Ellen Hinsey
The White Fire of Time
April 2003

ELLEN HINSEY (*b.* 1960) won the Yale Younger Poets Prize in 1996 with her first collection *Cities of Memory*. She teaches writing and literature at Skidmore College's program in Paris and the French graduate school, the École Polytechnique.

In this exquisite book-length sequence of visionary meditations, American poet Ellen Hinsey explores the boundary between poetry and metaphysics, and the intimate bonds between morality and mortality. A modern examination of the contemplative life, *The White Fire of Time* draws on a breadth of cultural knowledge and a deep understanding of the wisdom of the body.

This selection is from each of the book's three sections: *The World*, meditations on the ordinary, the daily life of the body and its place in nature and time; *The Temple*, investigations into language and the ethical life (XII echoes the medieval intepretation of Jacob's struggle with the Angel not as an encounter with an external divine being but rather the internal struggle of the self with consciousness); and *The Celestial Ladder*, poems tracing the soul's spiralling journey through desire, love, grief and endurance. Each section mirrors the structure of the whole, with poems following specific forms, serving to create a symphonic rhythm in which details, metaphors and meanings build and interweave.

I *Meditation:* On the Uncountable Nature of Things

I

Thus, not the thing held in memory, but this:
      The fruit tree with its scars, thin torqued branches;

The high burnished sheen of morning light
      Across its trunk; the knuckle-web of ancient knots,

II

The swift, laboring insistence of insects –
      Within, the pulse of slow growth in sap-dark cores,

And the future waiting, latent in fragile cells:
      The last, terse verses of curled leaves hanging in air –

And the dry, tender arc of the fruitless branch.

III

Yes, the tree's spine conditioned by uncountable
   Days of rain and drought: all fleeting coordinates set

Against a variable sky – recounting faithfully
   The thing as it is – transient, provisional, changing

Constantly in latitude – a refugee not unlike
   Us in this realm of exacting, but unpredictable, time.

IV

And once only a branch laden with perfect
   Fruit – only once daybreak weighed out perfectly by

The new bronze of figs, *not things in memory*,
   But as they are here: the roar and plough of daylight,

The perfect, wild cacophony of the present –
   Each breath measured and distinct in a universe ruled

V

By particulars – each moment a universe:
   As when under night heat – passion sparks, unique –

New in time – and hands, obedient, divine,
   As Desire dilates eye – pulse the blue-veined breast,

Touch driving, forging the hungering flesh:
   To the far edge of each moment's uncharted edge –

VI

For the flesh too is wind, desire storm to the marrow –
   Still – *the dream of simplicity in the midst of motion*:

Recollection demanding a final tallying of accounts,
   The mind, loyal clerk, driven each moment to decide –

Even as the tree's wood is split and sweat still graces
   The crevices of the body, which moment to weigh in,

For memory's sake, on the mobile scales of becoming.

XII *Meditation:* On the Struggle with the Angel

I

Suddenly, in the heat-weight of summer afternoon,
      When stalks of bleached grain near their sacrifice,

Knowledge tells you – *yes* – this shape that comes,
      Under the cover of beech shadow, by the stream,

You have met before; you swear you know this sharp
      Harvest breath – as once bending in shade you

Felt a presence near – or when from road-black light
      Shimmered once – and made one ask if all that

Rises invisible – disappears –

Or perhaps was it from the depth of a half-hewn sleep,
      When trailed by dreams you heard a fettered voice,

And waking quickly made your accounts – with *did* –
      Or *had* – in that ledger which hangs by night above

Your head, and details all your choices – *No* – you know
      This frame, which at close view could be yours –

The same—and resolute you square there, by the water
      As you had failed to do in those thatch-dark hours,

Though now, as then, you know yourself unequal to its
      Power –

II

For with a resolute strength it has found you out,
      Long-tired, it has watched you count out your sheaf

Of days, unable in the end to separate the chaff
      From the holy – but tonight, under the leafèd sky,

One more time you will try, and weigh this
      Weightless bulk against your back – locked together

You will stand, then – hammer, roll – lunge and
      Sway, until routed by its sure advance, reptant you

Will stagger back – but still hold fast to this frame
            Which could be no other –

And no more separate than the body to its breath.
            This angel – *now* – come to test your strength, knows

You part of the nature of beings who rarely rise
            To transcend the earth – and as such will fall too –

With the harvest of things.
            Still tonight – wrestle – face to face, pierce the gaze

That by you alone is driven – for alone you will
            Face its roar and fire, as you struggle to make good

With all that is given.

XX *Meditation:* On Feeling That the Dead Are Near

I

And when it seems that something rises beside you,
            The air tensed and still with what you cannot name –

And the familiar room itself seems afraid, bowed
            Beneath this thickening of moment – the silence rigid

And staid – you hesitate, at this apparition of all
            That is immanent, all that is essence, yet uncontained:

For rarely can one bear witness to that which is
            The release of all that indwells, free, its shell blasted –

So surrounded – stillness to stillness – you now
            Face that which is formless – though still somehow

Tied to the world, as if longing were the filament
            Which held it here – joined to the sphere of the present:

In this moment when edge to edge near, the regions
            Of being, non-being, the realm of the dead, anxiety

Flares: even if once you had wished for this coming –
            Or thought you had –

II

For day has watched you bend prostrate in rooms
        Where longing in countless details resolutely dwells,

And in midnight hours seen you uneasily pray,
        For the return of that one now only darkness-held:

But this presence is not the same nature as grief,
        Which is the will of the living – desiring the dead –

The dead too, have their tasks – their pilgrimage –
        And this is the Dead – willful – making their passage.

Your voice, hesitant, rises to speak: but untrained
        By qualities which would clarify presence, you ask

If it is love or mere hesitation which brings it back
        Here to the realm of the living: compelled by instinct

You manage a word, but language, dull instrument
        Is too blunt for the dead – and cuts roughly instead

The skin of the moment – and you fall, like a failed
        Hero, back to the stark wilderness of the material –

Where, your hand on the chair, you engage the bright
        Stare of the mote-filled light – in the breath-close,

        And stone-still rooms of the living.

ALICK NEWMAN

Philip Gross
Mappa Mundi
POETRY BOOK SOCIETY RECOMMENDATION
June 2003

PHILIP GROSS (*b.*1952) is a poet, novelist and playwright. *Mappa Mundi* is his first new collection since *Changes of Address: Poems 1980-1998* (from *The Ice Factory* to *The Wasting Game*). He lives in Bristol.

'The outstanding title-poem of this collection proposes lands more marvellous than the medieval cartographers imagined. It is a wonderful piece of lateral invention in itself. But it's also an apt flag-bearer for poems much concerned with the world-as-it-is. Philip Gross explores that world in all its quiddity and variety...Nature, people, the obscurities of one's self, yield up their otherness in those epiphanic moments when Gross's peripheral eyesight catches them off guard' – MAURICE RIORDAN, *PBS Bulletin*.

Walking the Knife

She looked out on her childhood garden; a late frost
had turned the leaves to knives. See the crack in the door
with the moon looking in? That's the knife.
The knife is no news of home on the evening news;
the knife is *waiting*, and a siren getting nearer in the night.

The knife is a straight street, glinting, sharp with rain;
it narrows towards the horizon; it can cut both ways;
the knife is no toy for a child; the knife-
sharpener looked in from the street as if he knew me
and when I said I had no knife he only smiled.

The knife is an old song that no one can translate now:
we walked three days without water on the plains of the knife:
even the word 'knife' might be not be right;
the knife is a letter that hides in the alphabet; dangling,
the phone flex is a species, cunningly disguised, of knife.

A package from the old world, sealed with tacky-tape
might be the knife they've sent for you, but how to open it
without the knife? Look, there's blood on the white
page – just a paper cut, so quick you never felt it;
the most innocent things can be friends of the knife.

The knife is lion-coloured mountains, seen through shivering acacias;
the knife is hunger in the middle of a meal with friends;
the knife is not *either*... nor *or*;
the knife won't take *No* for an answer... or *Yes*;
in the wrong town, on the wrong night, the knife is not a metaphor.

My mother's knife's handle was inlaid with lapis lazuli,
a clasp in the shape of a swan's neck; still it was a knife;
the knife is the last word: 'well?' And again
we're walking the knife edge, on towards the tip; if we
can keep our balance that far, we'll know what to do then.

Mappa Mundi

I

In the land of mutual rivers,
it is all a conversation: one flows uphill, one flows down.
Each ends in a bottomless lake which feeds the other
and the boatmen who sail up, down, round and round
never age, growing half a day older, half a day younger
every time... as long as they never step on land.

II

In the land of always autumn
people build their houses out of fallen leaves
and smoke, stitched together with spiders' webs.
At night they glow like parchment lanterns and the voices
inside cluster to a sigh. Tell us a story, any story, except
hush, please, not the one about the wind.

III

In the land where nothing happens twice
there are always new people to meet;
you just look in the mirror. Echoes learn to improvise.
So it's said... We've sent some of the old
to investigate, but we haven't heard yet. When we
catch up with them, we might not know.

IV

In the land of sounds you can see
we watch the radio, read each other's lips, dread
those audible nightfalls. We pick through the gloom

with one-word candles *home... however... only... soon...*
while pairs of lovers hold each other, speechless,
under the O of a full black moon.

     V

In the land of hot moonlight
the bathing beaches come alive at midnight.
You can tell the famous and rich by their silvery tans
which glow ever so slightly in the dark
so at all the best parties there's a moment when the lights go out
and you, only you, seem to vanish completely.

     VI

In the land of migratory words
we glance up, come the season, at telegraph wires
of syllables in edgy silhouette against a moving sky
like code, unscrambling. Any day now they'll fall into place
and be uttered. Then the mute months. The streets
without names. The telephone that only burrs.

Damp, Rising

For all our makings good, for a lick
and a promise of plasticky off-cream
gloss, woodchip on top, it smudges back
like a hurt round the eyes, like the dream

you gradually know you're in, again.
The autumn brings it up (the house
won't sell) like mist on long-drained
Levels, trees up to their knees, cows

legless, eerie-unconcerned, the ground
remembering its life as floodland,
and the M5 sunk, its undercurrent slowed.

Like that, or like a face beyond belief,
a poor exposure on the holy handkerchief,
the sweat-marked bedsheet of the Shroud.

Nin Andrews
The Book of Orgasms
June 2003

NIN ANDREWS lives in Ohio. This is the third
incarnation of her *Book of Orgasms*, inc-
luding pieces from two other prizewinning
books, *Spontaneous Breasts* (1998) and *Why
They Grow Wings* (2001), as well as a new
sequence, *The Pussy Talks*.

An underground cult classic in the States, Nin Andrews' *Book of Orgasms*
is a collection of playful fictions or prose poems, part human, part divine,
leaping from our everyday world to explore the limits of bliss: 'Borgesian
fictions, Swiftian sex...sheer euphoria, sheer poetry' (Rachel Jane Weiss).
She maps the imaginary terrain of that upper realm, the place where
euphoria endures. David Wojahn writes: 'There is no other young writer
– at least not on these shores – whose work even remotely resembles that
of Nin Andrews. To find her predecessors one has to look to Europe, to
the sly and sometimes erotic zaniness of Luis Buñuel.'

The Quest

Orgasms are bad news. In the town where I grew up, people didn't
allow them. They nipped them in the bud. Men and women dressed
in heavy black cloaks. On windy days they looked like dark sails on
the streets. By the time I was twelve, I wanted to leave. I wanted
an orgasm. Just one, I said. I knew it was a bad idea. Wise men
tried to convince me otherwise. They explained that men were
made in the image of God. We must live godly lives. God never
had orgasms. Neither should I. I did my best to remain orgasm-
less, but curiosity got the better of me. One day I felt one. Fresh,
alive, pungent. My soul left my body at once. Caught fire like
paper. Everyone knew. My face gave me away. Women took off
their gowns, opened white thighs that had never seen the sun and
positioned themselves in ways I never imagined possible. The
women were acrobats in disguise. I mounted them all. I was very
fast. Men were outraged. I had to run for my life. The people
stoned me. The gates of the city slammed behind me. Now I can
never return. I'm a disgrace to my name. All existence is suffering.
I am bewitched by orgasms. No one can relieve me from their spell.
I am doomed to wander the earth in an endless quest for orgasms.

The Ultimate Orgasm

For years I have been growing orgasms in a Petri dish. It's a costly and difficult task and would have been impossible without the expert help of renowned scholars whose lives have been devoted to the development and improvement of the orgasm. So far we have captured only a select number from the great variety available. When a volunteer comes into the laboratory, we do our best to describe the nature of our existing orgasms. We instruct and guide him or her on the proper courses of action, but it's impossible to know what you're giving a person. An orgasm can never be predicted. The orgasms come in many styles. Some are blanks. A few are silent and slip away without anyone knowing, making narrow escapes and blushing when you call their names. Others are scary. They use the body as a ventriloquist through which the stifled moans and tormented howls of cats and the murdered may be heard. Men think they'll die from the haunted orgasms. Women make no comment at all. But the best orgasms burst from a person like a cap off a Coke bottle and never come one at a time. These are the ultimate orgasms. When a person reaches the heights of the ultimate orgasms, we cannot contain our joy. We break open the champagne and cheer wildly.

Confessions of an Orgasm

When I was a mere slip of a thing, Mother taught me that orgasms can't tolerate humans, the scent of sweat mingling with perfume. When the time comes for you to enter a body, resist for all you're worth. Like the pilot of a plane circling over a city, looking down at the lights, remain airborne as long as possible, checking out the small lives below. When at last you touch ground, stay for an instant before taking to the air again, laughing as the pathetic people rush for their doors and cry out like abandoned children. No passengers are ever allowed on board.

Me, I love the pungent humans. I cannot resist their call. Like snow in winter, I fall helplessly, slowly, before dissolving into a river at the moment of contact. The loss of myself is always unbearable.

MOIRA CONWAY

Barry MacSweeney
Wolf Tongue
SELECTED POEMS 1965-2000
June 2003

BARRY MacSWEENEY (1948-2000) was born in Newcastle and worked mainly as a journalist. He won a Paul Hamlyn Award in 1997. *The Book of Demons* was a Poetry Book Society Recommendation.

Barry MacSweeney's last book, *The Book of Demons*, recorded his fierce fight against alcoholism as well as the great love of those who helped save his life – though only for three more years. When he died in 2000, he had just assembled a retrospective of his work. *Wolf Tongue* is his own selection, with the addition of the two late books which many regard as his finest work, *Pearl* and *The Book of Demons*. Most of his poetry was out-of-print, and much had never been widely published. The title is his. *Wolf Tongue* is how he wanted to be known and remembered.

'Barry MacSweeney was a contrary, lone wolf. For twenty-five years his work was marginalised and was absent from official records of poetry... MacSweeney's ear for a soaring, lyric melody was unmatched...his poetry became dark as blue steel, edging towards what became his domain: the lament' – Nicholas Johnson, *Independent*.

Pearl's Utter Brilliance
*(*FROM *Pearl,* 1995*)*

Argent moon with bruised shawl
discreetly shines upon my frozen tongue tonight
and I am grinning handclap glad.
We loved so much the lunar light
on rawbone law or splashing in the marigold beds,
our gazing faces broken in the stream.
Taut, not taught, being kept from school
was a disgrace, single word 'idiot' chalked
on the yard wall: soaked in sleet, sliding
in snow beneath a raft of sighs, waiting
for the roar of an engine revved before
daybreak, as the world, the permanent wound
I would never know in sentence construction, fled
away from my heather-crashing feet, splash happy
kneefalls along the tumblestones,
whip-winged plovers shattering the dew.

Each day up here I am fiercely addressed
by the tips of the trees; said all I could
while heifers moaned in the stalls, clopping
of hooves my steaming, shitting
beast accompaniment. And these giant clouds.
Pity? Put it in the slurry with the rest of your woes.
I am Pearl, queen of the dale.

Nil By Mouth: The Tongue Poem

(FROM *The Book of Demons*, 1997)

Demons, big-hatted and hard-hatted, far as gutter-toppled
squint-eye with grapple-lost spectacles can see, custard brain
head slanty on kerbside perch, vomit ready for a roller ride
into the X-rated, dog arse emptying unlit street, mongrel eyeing
the demon conveyors from here to eternity, bottle after bottle,
twisted cork to twisted head and unscrewed, screwed-up life,
over the slag heap of stonegrey aggregate from the moony saltpan
beds where the stones will surely lie upon my swollen liver,
as the swollen argent river sweeps across the tumblestones.
Grog demon biceps leaving me moan groggy, foggy-bonced,
pouring lunarstruck salt, sel de mer, coarse white pellets
scuttle-funnelled on MacSweeney's stuck-out begging tongue:

Tongue stuck out like raw begging hand in the mall, sticking
out straight, single digit filthy message signal up yours tongue,
in the air bloated for booze upright needle Cenotaph tongue,
grovelling, whining, soliciting, pleading, eyes imploring,
thirst, thirst, thirst, craveache, pinecovet, itchneedlust,
but on comes the salinating, saliva-droughting insult, Sahara
mouth an agony O, my Lot's wife tongue, rough orange fur tongue,
tongue examined by Dr Guo in needle room number two,
bladderwrack tongue late of the ebbingtide pools, salt on the rocks,
tongue of the deep sea trawler lick hull clean department,
tongue out on rent as a dog's public park hard-on, for
artists to paint in glory of its pinky stiffness and quality
as blotting paper for anything as long as it's a double on the rocks.

Blot, blot, blot, blotting me out: moan, moan, take me
from the slake tide to lake or snaky clean river, before
the endless chained pails of salt end me, tireless demons

happy in their work: a regular seven dwarfs scenario,
whistling darkly all the way to the daily saltbeds as
they pour, pour, pour, and the demons' capped gaffer,
fancy Dan Demon Man, who shall always be known as
the one with the Mouth of Rustling and Relentless Blades,
swaggers barely into focus from my throne in the gutter,
one hand filled with bottles and the other with scran.

Just one more, sir, for the road?

We Are Not Stones
(FROM *Pearl in the Silver Morning*, 1999)

Darkly-harnessed light will fall like a shawl
and be the hunky-dory
death of us all. A hawk-wing death,
a shrike strike death, a death in a lair.
This mossy path, frilled with feldspar
to prick your pearly toes, fresh from the marigolds,
the little stile not squeaking now, lubricated
hinges, hymns to the silence of adult interference,
new sunken screwheads glinty in sunlight,
the death of the white linen: our cot-death.
It was all, all of it, all for us, from the wonders
of our mysterious heaven
to the trout's opal seed-sac bubbling with jewels.
The water was anointment water,
a cool upland baptism. You, you
were Delilah and Mary-of-the-tears,
of the unspoiled lips lapping rushing whitewater.
Milton was a blind man and we knew nothing of him.
Paradise Lost to the ears of his daughter.
Where are they now, our camps of wild primrose?
Now we are adults too, all grown-up.
You're there, I'm here, miles from our happiness.
We are not stone, but we are in the grinder.
Everything is lost, and we are dust and done for.

Gwyneth Lewis
Keeping Mum

POETRY BOOK SOCIETY RECOMMENDATION

June 2003

GWYNETH LEWIS (*b.* 1959) is currently sailing round the world. She has published six collections of poetry, three in Welsh and three in English, including *Parables & Faxes* and *Zero Gravity* from Bloodaxe.

Keeping Mum is the latest book of poems in English from Wales's bilingual virtuoso. It is a psychiatric detective story which explores the effect of a dying language on its speakers and looks at how abuses of language might lead to mental illness. Her investigation begins with a police interrogation, then moves to a mental hospital, where the subject is questioned by a psychiatrist. Finally she uncovers angels in a sonnet sequence, messengers from another realm inside everyday lives speaking to us through depression and bereavement. *Keeping Mum* started out as a translation of Gwyneth Lewis's last Welsh book, but took on a life of its own.

A Poet's Confession

'I did it. I killed my mother tongue.
I shouldn't have left her
there on her own.
All I wanted was a bit of fun
with another body
but now that she's gone –
it's a terrible silence.

She was highly strung,
quite possibly jealous.
After all, I'm young
and she, the beauty,
had become a crone
despite all the surgery.

Could I have saved her?
made her feel at home?

Without her reproaches.
I feel so numb,
not free, as I'd thought...

Tell my lawyer to come.
Until he's with me,
I'm keeping mum.'

Mother Tongue

'I started to translate in seventy-three
in the schoolyard. For a bit of fun
to begin with – the occasional "fuck"
for the bite of another language's smoke
at the back of my throat, its bitter chemicals.
Soon I was hooked on whole sentences
behind the shed, and lessons in Welsh
seemed very boring. I started on print,
Jeeves & Wooster, Dick Francis, James Bond,
in Welsh covers. That worked for a while
until Mam discovered Jean Plaidy inside
a Welsh concordance one Sunday night.
There were ructions: a language, she screamed,
should be for a lifetime. Too late for me.
Soon I was snorting Simenon
and Flaubert. Had to read much more
for any effect. One night I OD'd
after reading far too much Proust.
I came to, but it scared me. For a while
I went Welsh-only but it was bland
and my taste was changing. Before too long
I was back on translating, found that three
languages weren't enough. The "ch"
in German was easy, Rilke a buzz...
For a language fetishist like me
sex is part of the problem. Umlauts make me sweat,
so I need a multilingual man
but they're rare in West Wales and tend to be
married already. If only I'd kept
myself much purer, with simpler tastes,
the Welsh might be living...
                                    Detective, you speak
Russian, I hear, and Japanese.
Could you whisper some softly?
I'm begging you. Please...'

Therapy

Did you hear the one about the shrink
who let obsessive-compulsives clean his house
as if their illnesses were his?
They made good caretakers, stayed up all night
rattling doorknobs, testing locks,
domesticated poltergeists.

He started an amateur dramatics group
with the psychotics, who had a ball
in togas, till they burnt down the hall.
Chronic depressives are always apart,
so he'd check them through his telescope,
placed them in poses from classical art

and, of course, they'd hardly ever move,
added a certain style to the grounds.
He recorded Tourette patients' sounds,
sold them to pop groups as backing tracks.
Whenever possible, he'd encourage love
between staff and patients. He had a knack

with manics, whom he sent out to shop
for all his parties, gave tarot cards
to schizoids so they could read their stars.
Perhaps he was flip with other people's pain
but his patients loved him and his hope
that two or three madnesses might make one sane.

Gwyneth Lewis's poems are included in two other anthologies published
by Bloodaxe this year: 'Mother Tongue' in *The Bloodaxe Book of Modern
Welsh Poetry: 20th-century Welsh-language poetry in translation*, ed. Menna
Elfyn & John Rowlands (April) and 'Therapy' in *We Have Come Through:
100 poems celebrating courage in overcoming depression and trauma*, ed. Peter
Forbes (June).

PETE BROWNETT

Annemarie Austin
Back from the Moon
July 2003

ANNEMARIE AUSTIN (*b.* 1943) has published
four other poetry books, including *On the
Border*, *The Flaying of Marsyas* and *Door
upon Door* from Bloodaxe. She works as a
tutor for the Open University and lives in
Weston-super-Mare.

Annemarie Austin's vividly imaginative poems open doors on other worlds
and other lives, drawing on her own memories and experiences, on art,
travel, dream, myth, history and literature. *Back from the Moon* begins
with poems of place and transition – a tunnel, an empty beach, an over-
grown quarry – inhabited by half-seen foxes, zoo animals undressing, an
infestation of swans, by long-haired men, Byron's lover Claire Clairmont
and Mata Hari, and by unreal princesses and angels dancing on the head
of a pin. But then it is cleft by the shock and tragedy of a father's ill-
ness, and finishes with a double sequence which speaks first of dementia
seen from the outside then invents a voice for a woman living inside that
condition (as in 'Pillow Talk').

Anne Stevenson writes: 'Austin is a fable maker. Hers is a poetry of parts
held together by powerfully imagined dream associations. As her world
deliquesces and reforms, her imagination breathes life into other people in
other times, weirdly authenticating the material she draws from history.'

Back from the Moon

When the Ageing Lady
got back from the moon,
her pockets were black with flour
that smelt of gunpowder.

She stank of moon,
of spent cap-pistol caps.
She was some veteran
of back behind the cannon

and leaked black drops
to pit earth dust with moon
like rain ahead of thunder
on the gutter's summer floor.

She told them: it's this
that accounts for moon,
that nightly luminosity
is lit gunpowder

and dark of the moon
the resultant charring –
a great burnt black matchhead
among the ignited stars;

I saw it up close;
my eyelashes were singed
by that white flaring,
then saved when the light went out

Pin

The Ageing Lady had come upon angels
who danced on the head of a pin.
I cannot tell you how many they were

but they shifted before her eyes
like slices of shadow,
like columns and trajectories
of moted sunlight;

all these writ small, of course –
she did not tell me exactly what size.
It was winter.
The cold made metal hard to bear,

except for these angels
whose bare feet bounced and bounded
from the freezing steel
in holy untroubled multitudes –

perhaps – if you could catch them
long enough to count them,
ensure it was not the same few whirling
over and over

disguised as scratches of light.
She closed a hand on them
and felt their electricity
prick up against her palm.

What should the Ageing Lady do,
handling this fizzing thing
like some dangerous live grenade
distilled down to its pin,

but take it up and fix it
to the collar of her dress
and carry the angels spinning
under her chin everywhere?

Pillow Talk

If anyone needs me, I'm sorry, I'm sleeping
whenever it is. The phone is ringing
at the other end of the ocean. I'm a whale.
I can hear that sound along deep-sea tunnels,
calculate its distance. A million miles.

We whales sleep upright like the wrapped dead
with weighted feet. Sometimes I lie down.
It is better than waking: the population makes
no demands, eating happens intravenously.
How simple this water where the bones float.

Peter Didsbury
Scenes from a Long Sleep
NEW & COLLECTED POEMS
July 2003

PETER DIDSBURY (*b.*1946) moved to Hull at the age of six, and works as an archaeologist. He won a Cholmondeley Award for *The Classical Farm*, and his last two collections were Poetry Book Society Recommendations.

Peter Didsbury's inventiveness, outrageous flouting of convention and subversive humour are fully displayed in *Scenes from a Long Sleep*, a feast of imaginative wonders by this 'secular mystic with the lugubrious tongue' (*Independent on Sunday*). Sean O'Brien writes: 'Didsbury's is the kind of work which makes you realise what you've been putting up with in the meantime. The product of a large and peculiar imagination, it shows a sense of adventure hardly to be paralleled in contemporary poetry.'

A Malediction

Spawn of a profligate hog.
May the hand of your self-abuse
be afflicted by a palsy.
May an Order in Council
deprive you of a testicle.
May your teeth be rubbed with turds
by a faceless thing from Grimsby.
May your past begin to remind you
of an ancient butter paper
found lying behind a fridge.
May the evil odour of an elderly male camel
fed since birth on buckets of egg mayonnaise
enter your garden and shrivel up all your plants.
May all reflective surfaces
henceforth teach you to shudder.
And may you thus be deprived
of the pleasures of walking by water.
And may you grow even fatter.
And may you, moreover, develop athlete's foot.
May your friends cease to excuse you,
your wife augment the thicket of horns on your brow,
and even your enemies weary of malediction.

May your girth already gross
embark on a final exponential increase.
And at the last may your body, in bursting,
make your name live for ever,
an unparalleled warning to children.

Owl and Miner

The owl alights on his shoulder.
All the day-shift she's waited patiently there,
high in the pine that grows hard-by the pit-head.
Waited blinking and dreaming,
and turning the slow escutcheon of her face.
Waited as that which would serve to draw her master
back with songs from his deep Plutonic shades.

Thus it is that he steps from the earth and is greeted.
She furls her wings, and as they set off
on their mile up the darkening lane,
towards the low-banked cloud of the clustering houses,
he starts to sing to her. I see his white smoke.
His breath on the air he casts as if he would net
the voices of ghosts in the empty elder trees.
For it is winter now, and his songs are of winter.
Wind unparcelled across the keen land.
First light snowfall turning black on hedge.
Warren and iron pool and far road-end,
where now the yellow lights begin to come on,
in twos and threes, haltingly, as if to conjure
the stars to commence their stammering nightly speech.

A Natural History

You spoke last time we met
of the petrol-coloured sea.
Our discourse began to look up.
All those present had dreams of ocean to tell,
while one of us claimed to have talked at length
with Thomas Hobbes, the author of *Leviathan*.

He'd been dreaming, he supposed,
was only partly convinced.
The summer then had not yet got under weigh
and all of us were desperately looking forward
to things achieving the balance they seem to have now.

What that means to you I can never know
but with me it involves the formal necessity
of the months of May and June, the fact of the gardens
which lie behind the street in which I live.

I can never know.
But I think it possible you will understand
the degree to which one can come to admire
the evenings at this time of year.
The swift-infested swooping of the dusk.
The sliding planes and opalescent
departments of the sky.

The Green Boy

At the moment of dawn
some long-ago May morning
a green boy emerges
glistening from this dock

stands dripping on the side
of this old stone basin,
and as the light breaks
gazes with newly opened eyes

at smoke lying curled
above one or two houses
in the city's huddled circle,
where the thin child servants

of lawyer and apothecary
of mountebank and thief
are up betimes
and about their masters' business

BERNARD MITCHELL

Peter Reading
Collected Poems
3: POEMS 1997-2003
September 2003

PETER READING (*b.* 1946) won the Lannan Literary Award for Poetry in 1990. His first 18 collections are published in the first two volumes of his *Collected Poems*. He lives in Ludlow, Shropshire.

For thirty years Peter Reading has been one of Britain's most original and controversial poets: angry, uncompromising, gruesomely ironic, hilarious and heartbreaking – as funny as he is disconcerting. He is probably the most skilful and technically inventive poet writing today, mixing the matter and speech of the gutter with highly sophisticated metrical and syllabic patterns to produce scathing and grotesque accounts of lives blighted by greed, meanness, ignorance, political ineptness and cultural impoverishment.

Bloodaxe also publishes Isabel Martin's study *Reading Peter Reading* (2000). This third volume of his *Collected Poems* includes the complete texts of *Work in Regress* (1997), *Ob.* (1999), *Marfan* (2000), *[untitled]* (2001), *Faunal* (2002), as well as a new long poem, *Civil* and a new collection, *ℐ* (its title is the printer's *delete* symbol).

from Civil

Prince Rupert's Cavaliers being victors here,
we and the town was subject to their pillage,
they then possessed our very homes and lives,
damning and cursing, threatening, frightening
our womenfolk with naked blades and pistols,
they picked our purses, sought out any wealth
they thought we might have hid in outhouses
and any other place they could suppose
we had concealed our modest stores and savings.
We was compelled thus to yield goods and money,
our women being robbed of chastity,
their impudent molesters bragging of it,
boasting of their lascivious lechery.
That night the plunderers did not retire,
but sat up revelling, robbing and raping.
Next day, with gunpowder and stocks of straw,
they fired our humblest hovels for their sport.

from 𝄞

Many malign pestiferous phlegm-slimes
writhed in this vile reptilian seething mass,
the stench of which induced faeces and vomit
(my chitterling voids, e'en now, to recollect,
until I swoon in etiolated terror).

Noosed in these scaled constrictuous twisting coils,
the naked vulnerable shrieked their spasms –
genitals gimleted by *Ophidia*
which exited from assholes, tied tight knots,
inflicted mass excoriating torture.

My Guide to me: 'Observe the eternal lot
of *sapiens*, whether he transgress or not.'

*

Oars of smoothed pine polished white by the waves of
    oceans shattered –
those of my crew whom I valued most were
    plucked from the gunwales
shrieking the names of their kindred as they
    hurtled gulfwards
(just as a skilful angler using a
    sliver of ox-horn
filed to a barbed hook casts out the glinting
    lure towards small fry,
tweaking them into the rocks to perish
    pounded and broken;
so were my boldest brothers snatched from their
    transient safety).

I have endured much on the whipped brine but
    never such raw grief.

*

Then the warrior-king, red-haired Menelaus,
    said to Telemachus:

Well, if you wish, then of course return
    to your father's fastness,

though I must tell you, three things are the
    duties of nobles –

first, a guest should be treated with honour
    while he is fêted;

second, a guest who must go should not be de-
    tained by some over-

sedulous shelterer (no one should be claustro-
    phobically clinging);

third, fine food and riches should swell the de-
    parter's chariot

(white-armed, high-born Helen will fettle spiced
    meats from our kitchens,

there must be wine, and, of course, this mixing-bowl
    wrought by Hephaestus…).

    Thus should a man take his leave;
    suitably sated, equipped.

Stephen Dobyns
The Porcupine's Kisses
September 2003

STEPHEN DOBYNS (*b.* 1941) is a leading American poet, novelist and crime writer. His poetry books include *Velocities: New & Selected Poems*, *Common Carnage* and *Pallbearers Envying the One Who Rides*, all published by Bloodaxe in Britain.

Stephen Dobyns exposes the bruised male ego in this innovative and wildly original book of prose poems, maxims and definitions (illustrated by Howie Michels). The barbed and wistful poems feature men looking back over past failures and successes, intercut with tart one-liners or "considerations" – like La Rochefoucauld's maxims brought painfully up to date. Dobyns' spikiest book ends with his own devil's dictionary in which his sharp quill pricks our pretensions, evasions and delusions by mischievously revealing the real, possible or covert meanings of words we use every day.

from The Porcupine's Kisses: *prose poems*

He had spent his youth dreaming of romantic triumphs, a world where his successes would be envied. Although he had no actual plans, he knew that his road would be made clear and so he waited, getting by on talent and saving his genius for when his name would be called. But no call came and life went by. What had he expected, that he should be unhappy now? Only in nostalgia did he roam through the rich place he had been promised, but the dream would end and again he would be left among cold streets, full of regret and resentment. Once he had painted the world in bright colors, now he painted it gray. But it was the same world, neither brighter nor darker, and when he vanished from its surface, the world kept on as before with no memory of his footsteps or desire.

*

He knew his vulnerabilities and concealed them: Nostalgia, naïveté, wonder. They could hurt him in the long run – inviting ridicule as sugar attracts flies. So every sunset, well, he'd seen better. Luxury, women, the routine frontiers of pleasure – he gave the impression that something was always missing. But deep inside he was the child singing alone in an empty room – chipped white paint and bare floors, late-afternoon light through a single window. Still, the concessions of adulthood had strained his voice his song was smaller – nothing like the symphonies he had composed when young, his astonishment's rich polyphony. And yet this present song – this melodic whicker, a groan of several notes, a droning bombination – what else remained to help him begin the day and accept those compromises which the day would force upon him in return?

*

His failures – could he blame them on time? He hadn't been ready when the lucky chance arrived. Or if not time, then perhaps the fault was how he reacted to time's upheavals – those surprises that seemed to come from nowhere. And often at the moment of success, the success was less than expected, smaller than deserved. So weren't his defeats the result of high expectations? He had worked hard, but the outcome wasn't what he hoped. Indeed, it was unfair. But who could say what was fair and what wasn't? Hubris, arrogance, self-love: wasn't it pride that said what he should have? What he had to have? Those setbacks – weren't they the result of an inner voice that said he deserved better, a voice that sang to him, soothed him and had never told the truth?

from The Porcupine's Kisses: *considerations*

It isn't yours till you can stand to see it break.

Repentant until he learns how to get away with it.

Only feels virtuous when seeking out the sins of others

He tried to make his children his second chance and they too turned out badly.

As his innocence diminished, so too did his willingness to love.

Hid by saying what others wished to hear.

By not believing in evil, he become its accomplice.

When he wants to insult you, he calls it telling the truth.

When he argues, other people's ideas show through the holes in his own.

Small talent; big smile.

Mistakes aren't the enemy; regret is the enemy.

Without his flatterers, where would be his genius?

By envying another's success, I become part of that success.

Howls at the moon; calls it music.

Sweet to its mate: the porcupine's kisses.

Every bad idea has a good reason.

Never found kindness because he first sought the meanness behind it.

She is angry he looks at her breasts; he is angry she gives him no place else to look.

Young, he thought the answers lay ahead; older now, he thinks they must lie behind.

Read books searching for the life he had hoped to live.

His wish to destroy was preceded by his wish to be right.

The first task of his self-deception was to hide all signs of self-deception.

Distrusted happiness because at such times he forgot who he was. This was also why he sought it.

Love doesn't need a reason; hate needs a reason.

When he is cruel, he imagines he was driven to it.

Calls his good luck destiny, his bad luck conspiracy.

When he begs your forgiveness, he believes he is doing you a favour.

The less he has to say, the louder he says it.

from The Porcupine's Kisses: *definitions*

Abyss: the dark from where you hear your name whispered.

Accommodate: conditional surrender.

Achievement: how long will he hang ribbons on the monster?

Age: not what you were promised.

Ambition: ladder made from the backs of others.

Ambivalence: cowardice in the abstract.

Anatomy: garden of earthly delights.

Anger: the fist I raise against myself.

Anxiety: four A.M. wake-up call.

Articulate: says what you wish to hear.

Authentic: convincing deception.

Autodidact: proud of his ignorance.

Beauty: reason's saboteur.

Behaves: puts his belly second.

Boast: seeks to add an inch to his small height.

Bountiful: to give unnecessarily.

Bray: the passionate articulation of second-hand convictions.

Bully: seeks outer validation of inner sophistry.

Camouflage: smiles.

Capable: untalented.

Carapace: academic tenure.

Pauline Stainer
The Lady & the Hare
NEW & SELECTED POEMS
POETRY BOOK SOCIETY RECOMMENDATION
September 2003

PAULINE STAINER (*b.* 1941) did not publish her first collection until her late 40s. After many years in rural Essex and then on Orkney, she now lives at Hadleigh, Suffolk.

Pauline Stainer is a poet 'working at the margins of the sacred', conveying sensations 'with an economy of means that is breathtaking...her poems are not merely artefacts, they have an organic life of their own' (John Burnside). *The Lady & the Hare* brings together poetry of rare luminosity from her five previous books and a new collection, *A Litany of High Waters* (from which these three poems are taken), all inhabiting an imaginative borderland inspired by her 'visceral Muse'. 'Pauline Stainer writes sacred poetry for the scientific 21st century. She is deeply English and draws from a wealth of sources: medieval lyrics, Eastern as well as Western art, Christian liturgy...But the subjects which engage her are always human, however referentially sacred or scientifically demonstrated' (Anne Stevenson).

The Hangar Ghosts

They come
as the hare dozes
in the dustless air

desultory
in their flying helmets
between huge drums of straw

silent, allspeaking
against the bruiseless blue,
as if the fuselage

still judders through
their bone-marrow
between sorties

and the sky,
serious with snow,
closes behind them.

Dreaming of the Dogger Bank

This was no dreaming act –

the waves came in
like grey wolves
without breaking stride,
over willow fish-traps,
through the fowler's nets.

Does the sea recall
how it lifted our ancestors
from their pastoral
at that last high-tide
of the known world?

Even now
when the waters reconsider,
you can sense deer
outpacing the shoals
through the driftwood of Dogger

and glimpse far down
the dripping rime,
the altered time,
owl and hare
in habits of bright dew.

The Thirteen Days of Christmas

On the first day of Christmas
a red rose is offered for the rent of Castle Rising

On the second day of Christmas
priests cast salt on the water in the shape of a cross

On the third day of Christmas
phalaropes walk in circles on the river-bed

On the fourth day of Christmas
the sagacity of beasts rises like vapour
through the turf houses

On the fifth day of Christmas
Christ sleeps on the pillow lava

On the sixth day of Christmas
six gentle falcons fall out of the sun

On the seventh day of Christmas
reindeer kneel in the interior

On the eighth day of Christmas
blubber lamps bob along Blubber Creek
to St Margaret's church

On the ninth day of Christmas
angelica leaves its signature in the fiery liquor

On the tenth day of Christmas
the best quill is taken from a swan's left wing

On the eleventh day of Christmas
eleven trolls are struck by sunlight
and turned to stone

On the twelfth day of Christmas
Mount Hekla lifts her cloud of unknowing

On the thirteenth day of Christmas
the last great auk comes up out of the sea,
flightless in the unforgiving light.

NOTE: In Iceland, Christmas Day is added to the traditional twelve days of Christmas. Mount Hekla, a volcano not far from Reykjavík, is often shrouded in vapour. The great auk's last major breeding ground was on Geirfuglasker, an island off southern Iceland.

JONO KNIGHT

W.S. Merwin
Sir Gawain &
the Green Knight

A NEW VERSE TRANSLATION
October 2003

W.S. MERWIN (*b*. 1927) is one of America's best-known poets. His other classic translations include editions of Neruda, Dante and *The Song of Roland* .

Sir Gawain & the Green Knight is a classic Arthurian tale of enchantment, adventure and romance. This splendid new translation – by one of the world's leading poets – has already been acclaimed in America. The original poem and W.S. Merwin's modern version are comparable in stature and imaginative power to another medieval epic, *Beowulf*, in Seamus Heaney's rendering.

All Camelot is merry with Christmas revelry when an enormous green-skinned knight with brilliant green clothes rides into King Arthur's court. This giant throws down a sinister challenge: he will endure a blow of the axe to his neck without offering any resistance, but whoever delivers the fatal blade must promise to take the same in a year and a day. When the young Gawain beheads him, the Green Knight grabs hold of his severed head and makes off on horseback. The poem follows Gawain's adventures thereafter – shockingly brutal hunts, an almost impossible seduction, and terrifyingly powerful adversaries – as he gallantly struggles to honour his promise.

Capturing the pace, impact and richly alliterative language of the original Middle English text – presented on facing pages – Merwin brings a new immediacy to a spellbinding, timeless narrative written many centuries ago by a master poet whose identity has been lost to time.

from Sir Gawain & the Green Knight

(two extracts)

The Green Knight takes his stand without lingering
And bends his head a little to show the skin.
He laid his long graceful locks across his crown,
Leaving the naked neck bare and ready.
Gawain gripped his ax and heaved it up high.
He set his left foot on the ground in front of him
And brought the blade down suddenly onto the bare skin
So that the sharp edge sundered the man's bones
And sank through the white flesh and sliced it in two
Until the bright steel of the bit sank into the ground.

The handsome head fell from the neck to the earth
And rolled out among their feet so that they kicked it.
The blood gushed from the body, glittering over the green,
And the knight never staggered or fell, for all that,
But he stepped forth as strong as ever, on unshaken legs,
And reached in roughly among the knights
To snatch up his lovely head and at once lift it high.
And then he turns to his horse and takes hold of the bridle,
Steps into the stirrup and swings himself up,
Holding his head in his hand by the hair,
And settles into the saddle as firmly as ever
With no trouble at all, though he sits there
        headless.
        All around him the blood sprayed
        As his gruesome body bled.
        Many of them were afraid
        When they heard what he said.

For he holds the head up high in his hand,
Turning the face toward the noblest on the platform,
And it raised its eyelids and opened its eyes wide
And said this much with its mouth, which you may hear now:
'Remember, Gawain, to get ready for what you agreed to,
And search carefully, knight, until you find me
As you have sworn to do in this hall where these knights heard you.
I charge you to make your way to the Green Chapel
To receive a stroke like the one you have given – you have earned it –
To be repaid promptly on New Year's morning.
Many men know me as the Knight of the Green Chapel,
So if you ask, you cannot fail to find me.
Come then, or you will rightly be called a coward.'
With a terrible roar he turns the reins,
Rides out through the hall door, his head in his hand,
So that the flint flashes fire from his horse's hooves.
No one there knew what land he was going to
Any more than they knew where he had come from.
        What then?
        Gawain and the King smile
        And laugh about that green man.
        All agreed that he was marvel
        Enough for anyone.

[...]

When they first heard the hunt the wild creatures quaked.
Deer dashed to the hollows, dazed with dread,
Raced up to the ridges, but all at once they were
Turned back by the beaters and their loud shouts.
They let the harts pass on, holding their heads high,
And the brave bucks too, with their broad antlers,
Because the noble lord had forbidden anyone
To shoot at the stags during the closed season.
The hinds were held back with 'Hey!' and with ' 'Ware!,'
The does driven with all the din into the deep valleys.
There might a man see the loosed arrows flying,
The shafts flashing through every break in the forest.
The broad heads bit deep into the brown hides.
Look! They cry and bleed, they die on the hillsides,
And always the hounds are racing at their heels
And hunters with loud horns following behind them,
Their shouts sounding as though the cliffs were cracking.
Whatever wild creatures escaped the archers
Were pulled down and torn apart at the dog stations.
They were harried from the high places and driven to the water.
The beaters were so skillful at the stations down there,
And the greyhounds so huge and hard upon them
They snatched them down more swiftly than a man's eye
           could follow.
      The lord, wild with joy,
      Would race ahead, then alight,
      Happy that whole day
      And on to the dark night.

C.K. Williams
The Singing

POETRY BOOK SOCIETY RECOMMENDATION

October 2003

C.K. WILLIAMS (*b.* 1936) is one of America's leading poets. He has published seven books in Britain with Bloodaxe, including *New & Selected Poems* (1995), *The Vigil* (1997), and *Repair* (1999), winner of the Pulitzer Prize.

C.K. Williams is the most challenging American poet of his generation, a poet of intense and searching originality who makes lyric sense out of the often brutal realities of everyday life. His poems present startling anecdotes and complex inner worlds, often using a distinctive long line, its worrying interplay of mind and measure following shifts of wayward thought and self-searching. They brood on love and death, war and violence, secrets, and human frailty.

In *The Singing*, his first book of poetry since the Pulitzer-winning *Repair*, Williams treats the characteristic subjects of a poet's maturity – the loss of friends, the receding memories of childhood, the baffling illogic of current events – with an intensity and drive that recall not only his recent work but his early books, published 40 years ago. *The Singing* is a direct and resonant collection: tough, candid, heartfelt, permanent.

The Doe

Near dusk, near a path, near a brook,
we stopped, I in disquiet and dismay
for the suffering of someone I loved,
the doe in her always incipient alarm.

All that moved was her pivoting ear
the reddening sun shining through
transformed to a color I'd only seen
in a photo of a child in a womb.

Nothing else stirred, not a leaf,
not the air, but she startled and bolted
away from into the crackling brush.

The part of my pain which sometimes
releases me from it fled with her, the rest
in the rake of the late light, stayed.

Oh

Oh my, Harold Brodkey, of all people, after all this time, appearing
       to me,
so long after his death, so even longer since our friendship, our
       last friendship,
the third or fourth, the one anyway when the ties between us
       definitively frayed,
(Oh, Harold's a handful, another of his ex-friends sympathized, to
       my relief);

Harold Brodkey, at a Christmas eve dinner, of all times and places,
because of my nephew's broken nose, of all reasons, which he suffered
       in an assault,
the bone shattered, reassembled, but healing a bit out of plumb,
and when I saw him something Harold wrote came to mind, about
       Marlon Brando,

how until Brando's nose was broken he'd been pretty, but after he
       was beautiful,
and that's the case here, a sensitive boy now a complicatedly handsome
       young man
with a sinewy edge he hadn't had, which I surely remark because
       of Harold,
and if I spoke to the dead, which I don't, or not often, I might
       thank him:

It's pleasant to think of you, Harold, of our good letters and talks;
I'm sorry we didn't make it up that last time, I wanted to but I was
       worn out
by your snits and rages, your mania to be unlike and greater than
       anyone else,
your preemptive attacks for inadequate acknowledgement of your
       genius...

But no, leave it alone, Harold's gone, truly gone, and isn't it un-
       forgivable, vile,
to stop loving someone, or to stop being loved; we don't mean to
       lose friends,
but someone drifts off, and we let them, or they renounce us, or
       we them, or we're hurt,
like flowers, for god's sake, when really we're prideful brutes, as
       blunt as icebergs.

Until something like this, some Harold Brodkey wandering into
    your mind,
as exasperating as ever, and, oh my, as brilliant, as charming, unwound
    from his web
to confront you with how ridden you are with unthought regret,
    how diminished,
how well you'll know you'll clink on to the next rationalization, the
    next loss, the next lie.

Doves

So much crap in my head,
so many rubbishy facts,
so many half-baked
theories and opinions,
so many public figures
I care nothing about
but who stick like pitch;
so much political swill.

So much crap, yet
so much I don't know
and would dearly like to:
I recognize nearly none
of the birdsongs of dawn –
all I'm sure of is
the maddeningly vapid *who*,
who-who of the doves.

And I don't have half
the names of the flowers
and trees, and still less
of humankind's myths,
the benevolent ones,
from the days before ours;
water-plashed wastes,
radiant intercessions.

So few poems entire,
such a meager handful
of precise recollections of paintings:
detritus instead, junk,
numbers I should long ago
have erased, inane
"information," I'll doubtlessly
take with me to the grave.

So much crap, and yet,
now, morning, that first
sapphire dome of glow,
the glow! The first sounds
of being awake, *the sounds!* –
a wind whispering, but even
trucks clanking past,
even the idiot doves.

And within me, along
with the garbage, faces, faces
and voices, so many
lives woven into mine,
such improbable quantities
of memory; so much already
forgotten, lost, pruned away –
the doves though, the doves!

JOANNA ELDREDGE MORRISSEY

Susan Wicks
Night Toad
NEW & SELECTED POEMS
POETRY BOOK SOCIETY RECOMMENDATION
October 2003

SUSAN WICKS (*b.* 1947) directs the writing programme at the University of Kent, and lives in Tunbridge Wells. Her first three collections were published by Faber.

Susan Wicks' poetry transforms the apparently ordinary into something precise, surprising and revelatory. The new poems of *Night Toad* move outwards from the intimacy of personal loss to a wider landscape haunted by disappearance, including a French Flanders still scarred by successive wars. The book also draws on her collections *Singing Underwater* (1992), *Open Diagnosis* (1994) and *The Clever Daughter* (1997).

Omens

A click, a gap,
a dead bird on the doorstep,
a cloud shaped like an angel
– and bit by bit
the airwaves swell and fill
with piped laughter; a slug
presses its pale belly to the pane.

A tendril of ivy taps,
a gutter drips. Bees wake,
eat their slow way out between bricks.

And then the walls are down,
every door open and swinging.
Wires snake across the hearth-rug
to the jump and flash
of strobe-light. Where there was moon

a rocket flares. A kiss of lipstick smears
a glass that isn't yours, a stain
unrolls its royal purple in the hall,
there's a pile of strangers' coats
where your bed should be; bodies
lurch and keel over, mouths blink off and on.

Night Toad

You can hardly see him –
his outline, his cold skin
almost a dead leaf,
blotched brown, dull green,
khaki. He sits so quietly
pumping his quick breath
just at the edge of water
between ruts in the path.

And suddenly he is the centre
of a cone of light
falling from the night sky –
ruts running with liquid fire,
cobwebs imprinted on black,
each grass-blade clear
and separate – until the hiss
of human life removes itself,
the air no longer creaks,
the shaking stops
and he can crawl back
to where he came from.

But what *was* this,
if it was not death?

Birds over Tonbridge High Street

From our cars
we watch them ride the air, their wheeling shape
escaping and reforming, bunched opaque
and thinned, their angled wings
transparent as they turn, suddenly
letting the light through. I squint,
trying to track them. But each single bird
is nothing, flies with the flock and turns
and flies again until it goes to roost
in a tight fist. Another hour
and I'll be at your bedside. By the chart

78

they wash you, turn you, while you grow
transparent, as the days
bring other deaths – a fall from a flight of steps,
a car exploding, mobile phones
thrown from a crumpled train. The dark ellipse
unskeins itself, remasses, pulses
its black heart, disperses,
fades to a shred
of smoke, comes back
a rippling flag of birds,
a dancing flock.

The Clever Daughter
(after a misericord in Worcester Cathedral)

For six hundred years I have travelled
to meet my father. *Neither walking nor riding,*
I have carried your heartbeat to him
carefully, to the sound of singing,
my right hand growing to horn.

Your head droops in a stain of windows
as we come closer. The man who made us –
hare and girl   will barely recognise
the lines his blade left: six centuries
have fused us to a single figure.

Clothed and unclothed, we shall reach him,
netted at his cold feet. But as he unwraps us,
my cloak-threads snagging and breaking,
I shall release you, your pent flutter
of madness. And we shall see you

run from his hands and vanish,
your new zigzag opening the cornfield
like the path of lovers, the endless journey
shaken from your long ears, my gift to him
given and yet not given.

Ann Sansom
In Praise of Men and other people

October 2003

ANN SANSOM (*b.* 1951) has written two plays for Doncaster Women's Centre where she has also worked as a librarian and writing tutor. Her first collection *Romance* was published by Bloodaxe in 1994. She lives in Sheffield.

Ann Sansom's poetry overturns the reader's expectations. Her poems often present human dramas in which people are seen as acting out their versions of themselves in their own fictions – what Stanley Cook called 'an authentic Northern mix of realism and imagination'. *In Praise of Men and other people* is her first new book for nearly a decade, a welcome return for a quietly authoritative, resiliently gritty poet whose debut collection *Romance* won her many admirers, including Simon Armitage: 'Naturally accomplished and instinctively organised poems…There is a maturity to her work, a sureness of hand…a freshness too, and a bareknuckle confidence.'

What friends are for

What friends are for, to stop you going out too far;
and counting on each other, we're already miles astray.
It's mild for March. We're here to say goodbye –
soon you'll be in Brittany for good, she's packed
for Adelaide. And so, a little drunk, reluctant
to go back, we're heading for the sea almost in step.

The drained bay's like smoked glass but soft
and each foot's lighter than the last. Nearer,
the long white crooked wall is only foam,
the dim black roar is tons of turning water, nothing more.
Horizon light, a rim of guesswork now, will disappear.

We're on a darkened balcony to overlook, say, Greece,
that first night with the tree rats and the mix of thyme
and cooling brick and goat. Or France, bleak dawn,
a sheet of mercury we broke and breasted through,
somewhere else like this, right on the edge of earth and safe.

In Praise of Men

Generally speaking, they know such a lot,
and tell you some, if they feel like talking.

So, it bothers me, that print – *The Beguiling
of Merlin* – how it's hanging, not quite straight

between the windows in the bedroom.
Lovely but unjustified, I sometimes think,

to pick a wizard's brain and leave him snared,
betrayed, condemned, petard, and by his own book

too. All that wisdom and turned to wood
by a wicked woman. It bothers me, generally.

Crossing the Nile

A hundred times or more I've crossed just here –
these iron struts that cut the iron Humber
into silver bits, this chunk of train
chunk chunk on slats to lead us in
to long flatlands of always mist and promised rain.

You've been a few years dead, big cousin,
and I haven't missed you much, but here
I always have you in the window seat –
And that, our kid, it's called the River Nile.
I'd thought it might be sea but I was young

and you were streets ahead. Profoundly deaf
and slow at school, you turned out wise and rich,
surprising everybody with a film star wife, a Greek,
who took your every word for gospel
on the strength of your blank face. It seems

you had a way with words, a way of making magic
out of fitments, long settees and space
when crowded three-piece suites were commonplace.
I'm always pleased to hear your thickened voice,
instructive, kind and half believing in the strange.

Nancy

That woman reared a tribe of pagans, my mother said,
and your father among them, knowing no better.
Until he married, of course, and shaking off his wicked mother
mended his ways and took to milk and Mass like water.
But we liked her, admired the corrugated hair,
the pearl-drop earrings, her fingernails a set of tiny pillar-boxes,
the sauntering high-heeled slippers where others trudged
in turbaned curlers, grey men's socks. And the language,
her neat painted mouth pulled down, regretful, prim,

And so I had to tell him straight, she'd say. *I told him
he could arseholes, for me.* Her final word on everything
from parsons down to royalty. Too bold by half, braving
the pit-top to tell the manager what he could do with his five bob,
refusing to stand for the Anthem in the Legion and barred *sine die*
for her favourite verb. *They can arseholes*, she'd shouted,
parasites, battening on the poor. As if the poor
were someone else, not here, not her with her debts
and her old scandals. (One Christmas Eve, she'd set off

for the butcher's and turned up next day with the goose,
legless, a disgrace. *I met some pals*, she told us,
You know how it is.) And how is it with thirteen kids
and weeks of strikes and a man who laughed and cried,
that pleased to see you back. How do you keep that fine hand fine;
the ring to the pawn, and in between – Monday to pay-day
it's cold water, black-lead, soda, and a sacking apron to wipe it on.
We knew nothing beyond your jokes, the birthdays, weddings,

parties lasting a week, you leading congas in the street,
your spindle legs tireless in the glassy shoes through your seventies,
your eighties. And then your daughters in their best colours,
clashing perfumes, the front room spiky with wreaths,
your quiet sons weeding out the lilies. *I'll not have lilies
in my house*, you'd said. *They're for the dead.
Any bugger dares to send me lilies. You know.
You can tell them what to do.*

Tatiana Shcherbina
Life Without
SELECTED POETRY & PROSE 1992-2003
translated by Sasha Dugdale
RUSSIAN-ENGLISH BILINGUAL EDITION
November 2003

TATIANA SHCHERBINA (*b.* 1954) lived for several years in France, before returning to Moscow where she works as a journalist.

Tatiana Shcherbina has been called 'one of the most significant figures in contemporary Russian poetry' (*Kommersant*). In her recent work the elegant and ironic narrator meditates on love, disappointment and loss against the backdrop of Russia's social collapse. While her themes are timeless, her settings are distinctly contemporary. She writes about films, make-up, TV, computers ('Ru.net' is a common Russian website address), supermarkets, the environment, and much else.

Shcherbina is one of a new generation of European-minded Russians, but her writing also reflects an insider's awareness of Russian society, often challenging its patriarchal and chauvinist attitudes. However, her poetry is not primarily political but literary, and she shows great versatility in different forms and genres, writing in French as well as Russian. Her playfully meditative essays form a perfect counterpoint to the sophisticated and self-aware poems in this edition.

Life without you

Life without you is neglected, ramshackle,
cheap and simply unapproachable,
nightmarish like a provincial grocer's shack,
frozen through in a light summer mac,
without feeling, without right of appeal,
and judgment-day, every second signed and sealed,
is boring botanist's countryside,
where the steppe is endless and the lone horseman rides.
Whatever I'm grafted onto – the rose
or the wild Soviet fruit-giver,
I'm always the horse, driven till it foams,
a match for the bodybuilder,
who builds up the biceps of self-will
and endures over and over
life without you, in discord, despair,
my lover.

Ru.net

The Russian Federation has ceased to exist,
Russia is no more – only Ru.net is left.
No more ABC, *aza, buki, vedi,*
neither Kostroma or Kamchatka survives.
WWW is the new reigning city,
'sites' are the settlements for all the trades:
there are those more established, where beyond the gate
a kilobyte circulates, bursting with news,
there are the sky-scraped ones, the portals
covered in banners' garish stained-glass light,
there are those more extreme, like the cliffs
where mountain people fight it out with knives
and there are whole settlements, too,
uninhabited sites on three floors,
beaches, where like sardines in a tin,
everyone gets a tan by the end of the day.
A little person squeezes into a chatroom
searching for the unbroken journey.
A hacker–hitman flings his bombs,
sends them in letters, hanging from the net.
And this is Ru.net: lines rushing madly,
no holes left in the spider's web.
The mice there clicking with their shoes
and squirreling away the gratis cheese.
Geographical might has fallen,
we have resettled along the lines of hosts,
where, at the height of a historical ball
the world was re-sited onto a screen
and glumly rests itself in a monitor-box.
We play with it, one by one, and how
society falls away – the same society
in which we played the fool and played at war.

'How can life'

How can life, for such a prolonged period,
change from being bearable to being a total bane,
when – it's not like it should be, Comrade God,
the weather, the environment, the men.
Even the dogs' barking – it's not those dogs
who caressed the ear so beethoveny, chopinish,
the grass drew into itself the act of love,
but that was real grass – not these hay wisps!
My Lord, it's like you're not mine, like you've given your word
retrospectively to the Southern tribes, thrown in the towel
with us, for whom, and, I mean this, Lord,
the further we go in the forest, the more the wolves howl.

Woman

I put on lipstick, mascara,
cream, different coloured yarns and threads.
Thousands of eyes become a scanner
which sees me in the fire, places me under a shower
or leaves me seated in a wicker chair in the garden,
the light filtering through the lace of branches:
the skin is a screen, it takes on the throng
of stars in the freckled sky. Words
cover me in their wool, it fluffs out
like a halo around the pointless roundness of my face.
I smile in answer, and feel uneasy.
Or I fight like a beast to the very end.

Osip Mandelstam
The Moscow &
Voronezh Notebooks
POEMS 1930-1937

translated by Richard & Elizabeth McKane
with introductory essays by Victor Krivulin

November 2003

OSIP MANDELSTAM (1891-1938) was one of the great Russian poets of the 20th century, with a prophetic understanding of its suffering, which he transformed into luminous poetry. *The Moscow Notebooks* cover his years of persecution, from 1930 to 1934, when he was arrested for writing an unflattering poem about Stalin; interrogated and tortured, he twice tried to kill himself. The Notebooks include that fatal poem ('We are alive but no longer feel') and present a shattering portrait of Moscow before the Great Terror. Ordered into internal exile, he later wrote the 90 poems of the three *Voronezh Notebooks*. Anna Akhmatova's poem 'Voronezh' describes her visit to the Mandelstams in 1936, when 'in the room of the exiled poet / fear and the Muse stand duty in turn / and the night is endless / and knows no dawn'. In 1938 Osip Mandelstam was re-arrested and sentenced to five years' hard labour for 'counter-revolutionary activities', and died that winter, of 'heart failure', in a freezing transit camp in Siberia.

'I can't hide from the chaos'

I can't hide from the chaos
behind the Moscow cab driver's back –
I'm hanging on the tram strap of these terrible times,
and I don't know why I'm alive.

Let's take route A or route B
to see which of us will die first.
The city huddles like a sparrow,
or rises like an airy cake,

and scarcely has time to threaten us from the street corners.
You do what you like, but I won't take risks.
Not all of us have gloves that are warm enough
to enable us to travel over the curves of whore Moscow.

[*Moscow, 1931*]

'We are alive but no longer feel'

We are alive but no longer feel the land under our feet,
you can't hear what we say from ten steps away,

but when anyone half-starts a conversation
they mention the mountain man of the Kremlin.

His thick fingers are like worms,
his words ring as heavy weights.

His cockroach moustache laughs,
and the tops of his tall boots shine.

He is surrounded by scrawny-necked henchmen,
and plays with the services of nonentities.

Someone whistles, someone miaows and another whimpers,
he alone points at us and thunders.

He forges order after order like horseshoes,
hurling them at the groin, the forehead, the brow, the eye.

The broad-breasted boss from the Caucasus
savours each execution like an exquisite sweet.

[*Moscow, 1933*]

'Eyesight of Wasps'

Armed with the eyesight of slender wasps,
sucking at the earth's axis, the earth's axis,
I feel everything that ever happened to me,
and I memorise it, but it's all in vain.

I don't draw and I don't sing,
and I don't play the violin with a black-voiced bow.
I drive my sting only into life, and love
to envy the powerful, cunning wasps.

Oh, if I could be compelled
by the sting of the air and the summer warmth
to pass through the worlds of dreams and death,
to sense the earth's axis, the earth's axis...

[*Voronezh, 1937*]

'If our enemies captured me'

If our enemies captured me,
and people stopped talking to me;
if they deprived me of everything in the world:
the right to breathe and open doors
and to assert that life will go on,
and that the people judge like a judge;
if they dared to hold me like a wild beast
and started to throw my food on the floor,
I would not keep quiet. I would not suppress the pain,
but describe what I am free to describe.
Having swung the naked bell of the walls,
and having woken the corner of the hostile darkness
I would harness ten bulls to my voice
and pass my hand through the darkness like a plough.
And in the depth of the watchful night
the eyes would flare at the labourer's earth.
Compressed in the legion of brothers' eyes,
I would fall with the weight of the whole harvest,
with all the compression of the oath rushing into the distance,
and the flaming years will swoop like a flock:
Lenin will rustle by like a ripe storm,
and on the earth, that avoids decay,
Stalin will destroy reason and life.

[*Voronezh, 1937*]

Gérard Macé
Wood Asleep

translated by David Kelley with Timothy Mathews
FRENCH-ENGLISH BILINGUAL EDITION
November 2003

GÉRARD MACÉ (*b.* 1946) is one of France's leading poets. This book brings together three series of prose poems, *Le Jardin des langues*, *Le balcon de Babel* and *Bois dormant*.

Gérard Macé's work challenges the barriers between poetry and the essay. This play between and within genres is essential to his writing – which has been called *essai merveilleux* – and draws on a questioning of language in its broadest sense. His fascination with dictionaries, grammars and glossaries leads him off on journeys in which the real and the imaginary are fused, but without being confused. He slips between words like a marvelling child constantly hoping that one day the world might be read like an open book.

A Detail from Hell

I

You give as good as you get at library entrances; you are led to the hall of lost footsteps by another you. 'First you go through a gilded doorway,' I had been promised, but my only memory is of worm eaten wood, the three steps and the long corridor you had to walk down without looking back under the gazeless eyes of the readers who, in spite of the instruction to keep quiet, continued whispering the paternosters of the dead – the low mass of words I already knew by heart at the moment I was given one book for another, a manuscript illuminated with silences in place of a story in black and white.

In the time that it takes a child to count out twelve syllables on his fingers before getting lost in the lines of prose, I am led across the catalogue room and through a concealed door to the lobby of the Forbidden Books Room. Before a mirror and an empty chair (the mirror in which Angèle V. lost her sight, blinded by the red lake in the middle of the salon), the author who used his initials as a signature and delivered nothing in his lifetime is making ready to read, or rather to cast into a shipwreck, as though he had the score of the *Flood* in front of him, a sentence which rolls without stop or comma, follows the path of the stars and the length of a large *in-folio* whose pages he turns without looking at them: the winter of his soul comes out in his voice, and the passion he has always put into avoiding story-telling and narrative so clear that he might finally lose his *little virile reason*...

In the starry tea he would drink after midnight there shimmers the reflection of another's madness: Littré glimpsing in a single verb a flower ready to drop, a head being severed and a few words splitting off – the thwarted rose, the violet and the stammer, a never ending list which continues its flight on other lips. Condemned to echo for having failed to love, their murmuring is so tenuous it was thought possible to enclose it in the narrow corset of a few vowels.

II

Through the window of the Forbidden Room, on the meadow where the everlasting flower and the knotwort grow with the ivy brought in by Paulhan, the house of conversation can be seen with its shutters closed – in days gone by an aviary (of words, of hieroglyphs and dreams), today a gaming house cluttered with tables where the reader turns up when his name is called and places one last bet in silence.

Although he has never shown more than his face (and his hands when they protruded beyond the material of the wide sleeves), when he comes round he finally leaves the chastity of the shadows: he lights the lamp and, turned towards the dead, paints his lips blue before starting to write. The real now forever widowed, the veil can fall back on the face of my double, paler than the memories I invent and more ancient than parricide.

The door is banging and I want to flee, but a woman selling second-hand fineries asks about my father whom she knew as a valet (past midnight, he would wait for the masters' return to take their coats), then she opens a mirrored wardrobe with winter suits and negligées: she watches over this cloakroom seen only in private (clothes of a shadow or a transvestite prince, a last moment of coquettishness before death) with the same jealousy as over the most precious manuscripts.

'It's Lazarus's laundry,' she confides to me as though it were a secret, but the laundry is not marked and I see Lazarus wandering in search of his name, which he has forgotten after three days' sleep. A bachelor raised from the dead, he dreams of his sisters' weddings and rolls like a child in the sheets of his first bed.

Wood Asleep

Castle of ferns, *asleep in a nest of flames*, the forest has closed in as she sleeps on a beautiful woman with an ebony face, a dead woman rouged in vermilion.

Virgin unknowingly pregnant, mother of daylight and the dawn which soon will awaken her, she sleeps dreamless and speechless at the heart of the half-open book, where the child who has just learned to read looks at her furtively, finger on lips, waiting for the kiss on the mouth.

He would like to tame the beasts with an edible heart, and thinks he can hear within him the *bird whose song makes you blush*, with hare-lipped tones and a voice half-hooting half-hissing between waking and sleeping, as familiar as poetry returning without warning with its rhymes and reminiscences: the bonus and the straight flush, double lilac on the edge of the meadow, the moon in a bilingual book. Poetry come to seek milk for the dead is startled away at the slightest confidence, and flees in a trice the house it haunts: a courtisan turning on her heels to hide the scar on her neck.

The echo coming from the Greek, the pebble at the bottom of the well have been enough for centuries to measure the reach of her voice. Before it broke preventing her from declaring her name – that of singer or spectre dishevelled by the air, by the wind rushing in between song and story.

Her lover who knows nothing of how she sleeps tells us nonetheless of illuminated nights, a living fur and a spelling where the words are joined up. The book of memory is an exercise book with margins embellished in red, where the hand of the child calligrapher wavers between wood and forest, brother and sister, suicide and death. At this very place, a little later, the reader slips a knife between the words.

Interpolation or caesura, the haloed heart of the dead wood opens up to memory tangled up in branches – the illustrated forest of childhood and the panelling of bedrooms: locked cabinets, fumbling in drawers in search of the futile, such as age-old coins or the ring that perhaps no one knew was lost – any more than the needle or the heel bone discovered by the archaeologist: was it the astragalus with its winged name, the invisible "padding" in a slightly lopsided sentence, or the redundant bone that trips up the species?

Denise Levertov
New Selected Poems
November 2003

DENISE LEVERTOV (1923-97), English-born, moved to the US in 1948. One of America's leading poets, she was also an activist who fought for civil rights and environmental causes, against the Bomb, the Vietnam War and US-backed régimes in Latin America.

This new, comprehensive selection of one of America's foremost modern poets draws on two dozen collections published over six decades. It replaces her earlier Bloodaxe *Selected Poems* (1986), and includes selections from the six later collections published by Bloodaxe in Britain, from *Oblique Prayers* to the posthumously published *Sands of the Well* and *This Great Unknowing*.

Eavan Boland: 'This generous selection brings news of Levertov's final achievement. Here we can observe, from poems which span the decades, how this most private artist became a great and abiding public poet. As we read, her superb language and wayward music burn themselves into our minds and memories. In every time there are just a few poets whose work – for its sheer lyric conscience – carries poetry safely into the future. Denise Levertov, as this book shows, is one of them.'

Living

The fire in leaf and grass
so green it seems
each summer the last summer.

The wind blowing, the leaves
shivering in the sun,
each day the last day.

A red salamander
so cold and so
easy to catch, dreamily

moves his delicate feet
and long tail. I hold
my hand open for him to go.

Each minute the last minute.

The Ache of Marriage

The ache of marriage:

thigh and tongue, beloved,
are heavy with it,
it throbs in the teeth

We look for communion
and are turned away, beloved,
each and each

It is leviathan and we
in its belly
looking for joy, some joy
not to be known outside it

two by two in the ark of
the ache of it.

'...That Passeth All Understanding'

An awe so quiet
I don't know when it began.

A gratitude
had begun
to sing in me.

Was there
some moment
dividing
song from no song?

When does dewfall begin?

When does night
fold its arms over our hearts
to cherish them?

When is daybreak?

O Taste and See

The world is
not with us enough.
O taste and see

the subway Bible poster said,
meaning **The Lord**, meaning
if anything all that lives
to the imagination's tongue,

grief, mercy, language.
tangerine, weather, to
breathe them, bite,
savor, chew, swallow, transform

into our flesh our
deaths, crossing the street, plum, quince,
living in the orchard and being

hungry, and plucking
the fruit.

ORDER FORM

This form can be photocopied. Or simply write to Bloodaxe
giving details of your order (see instructions overleaf).

QTY	AUTHOR/EDITOR	TITLE	PRICE
	BOOKS FEATURED IN THIS ANTHOLOGY:		
___	Nin Andrews	The Book of Orgasms	£7.95
___	Annemarie Austin	Back from the Moon	£7.95
___	Julia Copus	In Defence of Adultery	£7.95
___	Peter Didsbury	Scenes from a Long Sleep	£10.95
___	Stephen Dobyns	The Porcupine's Kisses	£8.95
___	Carolyn Forché	Blue Hour	£7.95
___	Philip Gross	Mappa Mundi	£7.95
___	Ellen Hinsey	The White Fire of Time	£7.95
___	Kapka Kassabova	Someone else's life	£7.95
___	Brendan Kennelly	Martial Art *paperback*	£7.95
___	Brendan Kennelly	Martial Art *hardback*	£14.95
___	Denise Levertov	New Selected Poems	£9.95
___	Gwyneth Lewis	Keeping Mum	£7.95
___	Barry MacSweeney	Wolf Tongue	£12.00
___	Gérard Macé	Wood Asleep	£8.95
___	Osip Mandelstam	Moscow & Voronezh Notebooks	£9.95
___	W.S. Merwin	Sir Gawain & the Green Knight	£8.95
___	Peter Reading	Collected Poems: 3 *paperback*	£9.95
___	Peter Reading	Collected Poems: 3 *hardback*	£20.00
___	Ann Sansom	In Praise of Men	£7.95
___	Tatiana Shcherbina	Life Without	£8.95
___	Ken Smith	Poet Reclining: *Poems 1962-1980*	£7.95
___	Ken Smith	Shed: *Poems 1980-2001*	£10.95
___	Esta Spalding	Anchoress	£8.95
___	Pauline Stainer	The Lady & the Hare	£9.95
___	Anne Stevenson	A Report from the Border	£7.95
___	Sarah Wardle	Fields Away	£7.95
___	Susan Wicks	Night Toad	£8.95
___	C.K. Williams	The Singing	£7.95

Order form continues overleaf...

ORDER FORM *continued*

OTHER 2003 TITLES FROM BLOODAXE:

___	Neil Astley	Do Not Go Gentle: *funeral poems*	£6.99
___	Maura Dooley	The Honey Gatherers: *love poems*	£9.95
___	Freda Downie	There'll Always Be an England	£7.95
___	Peter Forbes	We Have Come Through	£8.95
___	Elfyn & Rowlands	Modern Welsh Poetry	£10.95

TOTAL £ ____

Overseas orders: please add postage (see below) £ ____

ORDER FROM _____

ADDRESS _____

_____

_____

_____

_____

_____

PHONE / E-MAIL IN CASE OF QUERIES _____

Please send me the books listed above *(post free in the UK)*.
I enclose a cheque for £_____ made out to Bloodaxe Books Ltd.
Or: Please charge my Mastercard / Visa / American Express / Switch
(please circle which), including postage if overseas.
Switch issue number___ Expiry date __|__

OVERSEAS ORDERS: POST & PACKING
Please underline which service you require
Surface non-UK: *Add 12.5%*
Airmail Europe (inc Eire): *Add 15%*
Airmail overseas: *Add 30%*
Lower rates apply for orders over £100: please contact us for details.

Please send your order to *(no postage necessary in UK)*:
**Bloodaxe Books, FREEPOST, NWW 7470A, Bala,
Gwynedd LL23 7ZZ, Wales**
SALES TEL: 01678-521550   FAX: 01678-521544
E-MAIL: sales@pandon.demon.co.uk

Complete catalogues and twice-yearly new books brochures are also available.
Visit our website: **www.bloodaxebooks.com**